PROKEM

AN • ANALYSIS • OF

A • JAKARTAN • SLANG

Other Masalai Press Books

- *One Thousand One Papua New Guinean Nights: Folktales from Wantok Newspaper. Volume 1: Tales from 1972-1985.* Edited and translated by Thomas H. Slone. 528 pages, 8-1/4 by 11 inches. ISBN 0–9714127–0–7.

- *One Thousand One Papua New Guinean Nights: Folktales Stories from Wantok Newspaper. Volume 2: Tales from 1986-1997, Indices, Glossary, References, and Maps.* Edited and translated by Thomas H. Slone. 613 pages, 8-1/4 by 11 inches. ISBN 0–9714127–1–5.

- *Rasta Is Cuss: A Dictionary of Rastafarian Cursing* by Thomas H. Slone. 108 pages, 5 by 8 inches. ISBN 0–9714127–4–X.

PROKEM

THOMAS • H • SLONE

PUBLISHED • BY
MASALAI • PRESS
OAKLAND • CALIFORNIA
2003

Published by
MASALAI PRESS
368 Capricorn Avenue
Oakland, California 94611-2058
U. S. A.

First Edition, 2003

Publisher's Cataloging-in-Publication Data
Thomas H. Slone, 1960-
Prokem: An Analysis of a Jakartan Slang /
by Thomas H. Slone.
p. cm.
ISBN 0-9714127-5-8
1. Indonesian language — slang
2. Indonesian language — Dialects —
Indonesia — Jakarta — Morphology
3. Students — Indonesia — Jakarta —
Language (New words, slang, etc.)
4. Puns and punning
5. Indonesian language—Social aspects
I. Slone, Thomas H. II. Title

I wish to thank Dr. Henri Chambert-Loir who kindly provided extensive commentary on an earlier draft of this paper, and Dr. Walter Redfern who provided helpful information to me. I am also grateful to several Indonesian students who provided me with Prokem examples and explanations.

Table of Contents

Introduction

The term ludling (literally, "play-language") was coined by Laycock (1972: 61) to mean a language that is created from an ordinary language "as the result of a transformation or a series of transformations acting regularly on an ordinary language text, with the intent of altering the form but not the content of the original message, for purposes of concealment or comic effect." As such, ludlings exist as a subset of play languages, namely those that are formed by regular transformation of a standard, base language. Ludlings as well as most other slang languages retain the grammar of the base language.

Ludlings occur in many languages throughout the world (Laycock 1972; Gandour 1978; Lefkowitz 1991: 11-30) and throughout Austronesia (Simons 1982). In English, the most well known ludling is usually called, "Pig Latin." Pig Latin words are usually formed by taking a standard English word, transposing the initial part of the word to the end, then adding "ay" to the end of the word. E.g., "scram" becomes "amscray." For words in which the initial sound is a vowel, the rule varies by nationality (Laycock 1972: 26-27, 42).

Prokem is a slang language that is spoken in Jakarta, primarily by youth who speak the Jakartan dialect of Indonesian. It most likely originated as a secret criminal language, but is today spoken by both high school and university students and by members of street gangs, *preman*, from which the name Prokem comes.

Prokem falls roughly within Laycock's definition of ludling above, in so far as it is secretive and it has many regular transformations, but it also contains non-regular transformations: redefinitions, acronyms, and new coinages. Furthermore, the regular transformations are not applied predictably, as appears to be true for most ludlings. The most frequent Prokem transformation is the "ok" infix transformation, and the majority of Prokem words are formed via ludic[1] (regular) transformations.

Slang is an encapsulated form of folklore; it is spoken by the "folk" (or common people), often without regard to standard grammar or with regard for obscenity (e.g. see Brunvand, 1968: 28-37). This encapsulation is evident in ethnic labeling, e.g. the Prokem *CABO* (whose Indonesian meaning is "whore" but whose Prokem meaning is "young hot pepper", implying someone from Minangkabau) or the German dialectical *Polsche* ("Polish woman" or "slut" [Roback, 1944: 110]). Folklore acts as a transmitter of culture, and as a psychological release. "As with all jokes, lies, parables, and other fiction, the teller visibly reveals himself in the choice of his subjects and in his special handling of them." (Legman 1975: 30; see also Malinowski, 1927: 98-120; Dundes, 1980: 54, 70) Culture-specific folklore also acts as a validation of culture-specific psychology. The existence of a folk item

---

[1]"Ludic" is the adjectival form of "ludling."

better indicates validity in the wider culture than do the results of the psychoanalysis of a single person. For example, Abraham (1927: 362-363) reports an analogy found between dirt and money in the psychoanalysis of his patients. Dundes and Pagter (1987: 67-68) and Legman (1964: 186, 388-389; 1975: 917-920) have found several instances of folklore equating money with shit. There are two Prokem examples that are comparable: *aring* (meaning, "expensive" in Prokem and "to stink" in Indonesian [Amien, 1988: 2]) and *tabung* (meaning, "to shit" in Prokem and "money box" in Indonesian [Rahardja and Chambert-Loir, 1990: 105]). This indicates that the equivalency is culturally widespread and not restricted to the psychologically disturbed.

Oral folklore is only transmitted so long as it has meaning and function (Legman 1975: 15-16; Dundes, 1987:vii). This is somewhat less true for slang, since individual words tend to evolve such that the original meaning becomes obscure to the current speakers. For example, few English speakers today would recognize that the exclamation "For crying out loud!" was euphemistic for the tabooed "For Christ's sake!" (Allan & Burridge 1991: 39; Hughes 1991: 13-15). "For crying out loud!" still functions as an exclamation, but no longer functions as a euphemism, hence it has lost its original meaning. Similarly, Prokem speakers may use words for which they do not know the hidden (euphemistic) meanings only because they know the current meanings (which is sufficient). This is probably true of some Prokem acronyms, because there are so many of them in standard Indonesian (e.g. see Mörzer Bruyns 1970; Kasim and Sinaga, 1989) as well as in Prokem. Similarly, most speakers are not aware of the different ludic transformations, according to Chambert-Loir (1984: 112). This is analogous to knowing how to speak grammatically without knowing how to describe the grammar, indicating as one would expect that Prokem is learned organically, not formally.

Methods

Data on Prokem was collected from three primary sources: Rahardja and Chambert-Loir (1988; 1990), Amien (1988), and Pur (1989). Two additional Prokem words were collected from Dreyfuss (1983) that were not in these sources: *Cokan* (from the Indonesian *Cina*, "China" or "Chinese"), and *Madokur* (meaning the island of Madura or Madurese). Table 1 lists a few words and definitions that were collected from university student Prokem speakers that were not listed in published sources.

Danandjaja (1988) refers to examples of acronyms as *teka-teki* ("riddles"), because that is the form in which they are often communicated. For example, in response to the riddle, "What does *MBA* [Master of Business Administration] mean?", he recorded two joke meanings: "Master by Accident" and "*Masih belum apa-apa*." ("Still nothing."). Rahardja and Chambert-Loir (1990: 165) reported the former as Prokem; the latter has not been reported as Prokem. This ambiguity leads to several possible interpretations as to whether each meaning: 1) is exclusively part of the Prokem lexicon, 2) was at one time part of Prokem but has reached broader usage, or 3) never was part of Prokem.

Table 2 summarizes the categories of ludic transformations based on Laycock (1972), who described them nearly exhaustively. Table 2 also summarizes non-ludic transformations that occur in Prokem. The table includes: 1) examples from Prokem dictionaries for each category reported by Laycock, and 2) a few examples of non-Prokem ludlings described later in this text. For each type of ludling in the table, a description of the corresponding generative grammar is shown when an example exists in an Indonesian or Malaysian ludling, and an example from the dictionary when such exists in Prokem.

A generative grammar is a method of defining a language from formulaic transformations. Its use is particularly apt for defining ludlings since ludic languages are formed in a highly regular manner and are hence easily defined in terms of simple formulas. In Table 2, the Indonesian words from which Prokem words are derived are given on the left side of each arrow ($\rightarrow$), the resulting Prokem words are given on the right side. Definitions of the symbols used in the formulas are given in footnote "a" of Table 2. A more complex description of generative grammars is given in Chomsky and Halle (1968: 390-399), as well as the application of generative grammars to Pig Latin (Chomsky & Halle 1968: 342-343).

Combining all sources of Prokem data, there are 4403 words and phrases reported in the lexicon with 4980 total definitions. Rahardja and Chambert-Loir (1988; 1990) reported 730 definitions that were not reported elsewhere, Amien (1988) reported 837 definitions that were not reported elsewhere, and Pur reported (1989) reported 1787 definitions that were not reported elsewhere. Chambert-Loir (personal communication) stated that Pur (1989) should be used with greater caution than Amien (1988), and so the greater number of unique definitions in Amien (1988) would seem to bear him out.

Two separate processes transmit words through time in Prokem: a ludic process that is primarily context (or word) independent, and a non-ludic process in which individual words are transmitted. For example, the Prokem word *bedokel* is one of many that is created by inserting "ok" into an existing Indonesian word (*bedel*, "operation"). Consequently, as Prokem has been evolving, all of the words using this infix are transmitted simultaneously and concisely. It is not the meaning of these words that is relevant, but the process, since "ok" can be inserted into almost all words, Indonesian or not. In contrast, an acronym, such as the Prokem *SIKONDOM* is transmitted in isolation because its meaning is dependent upon the current meaning of its component words. As its component words become archaic, so does the transformation become archaic. Furthermore, since *SIKONDOM* is meaningful both as Prokem and as Indonesian (*si kondom* in Indonesian [meaning approximately "Brother Condom"]; and *situasi, kondisi and domisili* in Prokem ["situation, condition and domicile"]), it is hence a humorous play on words, its tendency towards archaism is increased since humor is dependent on currency.

Words formed by ludic formations tend to be created with simple transformations, because a complex transformation process slows and burdens conversations (as suggested by Wentworth and Flexner 1975: 606-608). However, ludic transformations often but not always increase the length of words, e.g. the pure expansion forms (Table 2, part A). Non-ludic slang tends to be concise; it is in fact this conciseness that makes slang popular (Wentworth & Flexner 1975: x).

Regarding the origin of Prokem, Chambert-Loir (1984: 115) wrote that Prokem "emerged among gangsters and convicts and then became the argot of the street kids [*preman*]… In the early [19]60s, clearly, it already existed, perhaps it had already existed for some time before that. A number of people have claimed that [Prokem] first appeared in Medan [north-east Sumatra]. Perhaps street kids from Medan played a role in spreading it to the capital. In any case, the street kids are the intermediary group which has been transferring [Prokem] from the criminal group to the student group, and this phenomenon seems to have begun around 1970. In the late [19]60s [Prokem] was already being used by youths accustomed to taking drugs, but only after 1975 did the language begin to spread widely among the youth in the capital [Jakarta]."

This statement on the origin of Prokem contains several assertions or speculations, two of which are examined below: that Prokem may have originated in Medan, and that Prokem originated with criminals.

To find a likely origin of Prokem, it is necessary to: 1) examine the etymological origins of the words from which Prokem is derived, 2) examine the patterns of other ludlings in Indonesia and Malaysia, and 3) examine the historical relationship between modern-day Jakarta and rest of the Indonesian-Malaysian region.

Four methods have been employed to make Prokem secret from outsiders: 1) coining of new words, 2) euphemism and pun ($\{O\}$ in Table 2), 3) ludic transformation (e.g. $\{Ti_1\}$), and 4) acronym formation $\{\_\}$. The first method is not possible to analyze because it is generally not possible to distinguish new coinages from other methods with obscure origins. Ludic transformations can be combined as multiple transformations for greater secrecy (e.g. $\{ok_1+Ts_1\}$); and the combination process potentially indicates a relative temporal difference between Prokem words. For example, if the $\{ok_1\}$, $\{Ts_1\}$, and $\{ok_1+Ts_1\}$ transformations all exist in a language, it is necessary that the $\{ok_1\}$ and $\{Ts_1\}$ transformations preceded the existence of the $\{ok_1+Ts_1\}$ transformation in the history of the language. However, a specific word formed by the $\{ok_1\}$ or $\{Ts_1\}$ transformation may be newer than a specific word formed by the $\{ok_1+Ts_1\}$ transformation because not all aspects of language evolve sequentially.

Two pairs of subjects are interesting to analyze statistically with regard to secrecy (obscurity): 1) sex vs. violence words and 2) criminal vs. non-criminal words. An analysis of the former could indicate whether there is any difference in taboo value. An analysis of the latter could verify whether crime-related words did enter Prokem prior to other words. To remove possible problems of statistical dependency, words that fall into multiple subject categories have been removed from the analyses. Similarly, words that have an uncertain transformation have been removed from analyses.

Results

1. Etymology

Many languages of Indonesia are closely related. For example, Madurese, Minangkabauese, and Indonesian are all from the Malay group of languages; furthermore, many words from Madurese and Indonesian have entered Javanese (Horne 1974; Foley 1983a; 1983b; Mardiwarsito, Adiwimarta, & Suratman 1985). Indonesian is derived from proto-Malay in Sumatra and has had many additions from both indigenous and external languages, so it is sometimes difficult to discern precise etymology. Since the Jakartan dialect of Indonesian is the principal language of Jakarta, it is reasonable to assume that when a Prokem word is derivable from Indonesian as well as another language that it is most likely from standard Indonesian or the Jakartan dialect.

The languages from which Prokem words are derived are, in order of frequency (with approximate percents in parentheses): Indonesian (96.5%), English (1.5%), Javanese (1%), Balinese (0.8%), Sundanese (0.4%), Madurese (0.2%), Arabic (1 word with certainty), the Medan/ Deli dialect of Indonesian (1 word), Minangkabauese (1 word), German (1 word, *zwei-zwei* [Prokem, *zwai-zwai*; English, "in pairs"]), and Hawaiian Pidgin English (1 word, *pakalolo* [see Table 3]). These percentages do not add up to 100%, since some words are derivable from more than one language. For example, the Prokem *bulis* is derived from *pulisi* ("police") which is a word in both Javanese and Madurese; the Indonesian equivalent is *polisi*, and is hence a less likely derivation.

English words have entered Prokem due to its place as an international language and due to the importance it is given in Indonesian higher education. Some unusual words that entered Prokem from English are given in Table 3.

One word has certainly entered Prokem from Arabic: bahlūl ("stupid", "drunk/ intoxicated"). Amien (1988) reported three others, but these have been disputed by Chambert-Loir (personal communication). The disputed words are: *ḥarâmî–y* (Prokem, *haromi*; English, "to steal, thief" [Amien 1988: 17]), *marîd* ("sick" [Amien 1988: 31]), *tamr* ("date palm" [Amien 1988: 54]).

The German word, *zwei-zwei*, may have entered Prokem from tourists. It is an oddity, but indicative of the decline of the Dutch language in Indonesia today. The Prokem word *zwai-zwai* did not originate from Dutch, the Dutch equivalent is *twee-twee*. No Dutch words have entered Prokem directly, only with Indonesian as an intermediary (e.g. the word *prokem* itself is derived from Dutch, but only by way of Indonesian). Few, if any, words have entered Indonesian from Dutch since the revolutionary era.

The etymological influence from Sumatra (the Medan/Deli dialect of Indonesian and Minangkabauese) is very minor (Table 4). The claim that Prokem was derived from Sumatra is implausible based on this evidence.

2. Comparison with Other Ludlings

Table 5 lists all ludlings from Indonesia, Malaysia and Brunei that have been described. It is notable that several ludlings share transformation methods with Prokem (these are in **boldface** in the table). However, since Prokem has many different transformation methods, this is not surprising. There are 19 transformations in Prokem that utilize the {ong} and {cong}; these are most likely from the Jakartan *Bencong* ludling of transvestites and transsexuals, however only 4 of these definitions refer to transvestitism or homosexuality. Pur (1989) listed 20 additional {ong} transformations, indicating less discrimination as to what is and is not Prokem. The other Jakartan ludling, used by homosexuals, does not appear to have influenced Prokem since there are no {CSS} transformations in Prokem.

Most papers on ludlings report few actual examples. Of those non-Javanese ludlings in Indonesia, Malaysia or Brunei, only Evans (1917; 1923: 276-277) reported words that overlap with Prokem. This ludling called Cakap Balik (literally, "reverse words") was reported in the Negri Sembilan State of Peninsular Malaysia. Like Prokem and unlike the vast majority of ludlings, Cakap Balik was polysystemic (Evans 1917: 115; Laycock 1972:

81). Cakap Balik was "used by bad mannered Malay children when they wish[ed] to talk secrets before their elders and betters or before uninitiated companions." (Evans 1917: 115) This is true to some extent for Prokem, but also for many other ludlings as well (e.g. Pig Latin). Table 6 presents the words in common between Prokem and Cakap Balik.

The Minangkabau of northwest Sumatra, who have been characterized as having a strong wanderlust, began migrating to Negri Sembilan as early as the 14th century, where they are now the predominant ethnic group (de Josselin de Jong 1922: 9; Winstedt 1934; Naim 1973: 16). The Minangkabau of Sumatra and the people of Negri Sembilan have been "totally independent of one another" (de Josselin de Jong 1922: 165) since 1824 when an Anglo-Dutch treaty delineated national boundaries in Asia (Hall 1981: 549-551). But, Cakap Balik differs from the two reported Minangkabau ludlings (Table 5). Chambert-Loir (1984: 109) described these as single-rule ludlings that would probably be categorized under "conditioned suffix to syllable" using Laycock's (1972) system {CSS}. In contrast, Cakap Balik was described as polysystemic (Evans 1917: 115).

It is noteworthy that only 2 of the 8 words are from a single source of published Prokem data (*belih/beleh* and *guming*). That most of these words have been collected from more than one source indicates either that somehow these ludic transformations come "naturally" to the Indonesian or Malay speaker, or that there is an ancestral relationship between Cakap Balik and Prokem. Furthermore, because Pur (1989) and Amien (1988) each uniquely contributed a word, it gives some vindication to the validity of their efforts (see Section 2), since they were unlikely to have known about the work of Evans (1917; 1923) which has not previously been referred to in publications dealing with Prokem.

3. Sociolinguistic History

Old Malay began in southern Sumatra and spread during the 7th through 9th centuries with the Sriwijaya Kingdom (Osman 1986: 3). Modern Malay began functioning as a lingua franca (or trading language) during the 13th or 14th centuries when it was disseminated throughout the Indonesian archipelago with the spread of Islam (Osman 1986: 2-3). Sumatra had early and substantial trade contact with both China and India (Hall 1981: 47-48) and has served as a gateway between Indonesia and the rest of the world.

Jakarta is situated near traditional areas of both Sundanese and Javanese speakers on the island of Java (Foley 1983). Batavia (the pre-independence name of Jakarta) was established by the Dutch in the early 17th century (Abeyasekere 1989: 9-11), and the Malay language (i.e., proto-Indonesian) was used in Batavia from early times (Osman 1986: 4). Batavia was divided into many villages (*kampung*) for security reasons by the Dutch, each village was for one of the ethnic groups that lived in the city (Abeyasekere 1989: 30-31). The Bugis, for example, were given their own *kampung* in 1663 (Abeyasekere 1989: 31); similarly, there were Malays (i.e., from peninsular Malaysia) and Makassars in Jakarta in the 1600s (Abeyasekere 1989: 20,29). At the end of the 1700s, Malay was firmly established as the dominant language of Jakarta (Abeyasekere 1989: 33). "By the 1820s, however, intermixing had gone so far that observers could no longer divide the Indonesian community into distinct ethnic groups." (Abeyasekere 1989: 65) Though some ethnic divisions between *kampung* have persisted in recent times (Castles 1967; Abeyasekere 1989: 236). It was at this point (the 1820s) that a distinct Jakartan dialect began to develop (Abeyasekere 1989: 65). From the 1820s through today, Jakarta has been "a melting pot", attracting peoples from throughout the archipelago (Castles 1967; Abeyasekere 1989: 31-33,191). Beginning in 1901, the Dutch government began expanding its educational facilities in Indonesia, and subsequently brought students from various parts of the archipelago to be educated in Jakarta (Abeyasekere 1989: 94-97).

The Minangkabau were relative latecomers to Jakarta, whose population was only about 7000 in 1930 (Naim 1973: 169). However, prior to 1930, the largest portion of students in medical and law schools from "outer islands" were Minangkabau (Naim 1973: 169). The Minangkabau did not immigrate to Jakarta in substantial numbers until after independence; the number of Minangkabau in Jakarta in 1971 was estimated to be as high as 500,000 (10% of Jakarta) [Naim 1973: 169-170].

As noted earlier, the Minangkabau colonized Negri Sembilan in peninsular Malaysia beginning in the 14th century. However, the descendants of the first Minangkabau who emigrated to Negri Sembilan in Malaysia now primarily regard themselves as Malaysian (Naim 1973: 210). And, with the exception of Minangkabau emigration to Negri Sembilan, it is probably not possible to discern how great an emigration of Sumatrans there has been to peninsular Malaysia prior to this century (Naim 1973: 209-210).

The Javanese who migrated to the Deli area of Sumatra in colonial times as contract laborers primarily did not return to Java after their contracts ended (Pelzer 1978: 61), and so they could have only been a minor or indirect influence on the development of Prokem.

So, if Prokem was derived directly from an external area, such as the Malay Peninsula or Indonesian islands other than Java, two events make the cut-off date likely to be prior to 1830: 1) the Anglo-Dutch treaty of 1824 which greatly reduced communication between Malaysia and Indonesia and 2) the cultural homogenization of Batavia that began in the 1820s. Jakarta has always had immigrants from other islands, so small linguistic contributions from these islands have always been made to Jakartan speech. A large contribution to Jakartan speech, such as an entire slang or secret language, becomes unlikely after cultural homogenization, since the language would be that of outsiders and would be used as an ethnically-based exclusionary language.

The few Minangkabau who lived in Batavia prior to independence were primarily students and/or from the elite (Naim 1973: 169). Since it is believed that Prokem did not become a student language until the 1960s, and it is probable that Prokem was a criminal language previous to this (see Section 3.5), it is unlikely that there could have been a significant Minangkabau contribution to the Prokem prior to independence.

4. Puns

The pun is perhaps as poorly defined in English as it is in Indonesian. Nonetheless, English distinguishes the pun as a subset of word play whereas Indonesian does not (*permainan kata-kata* means "word play" or "pun"). However, the concept of pun as a sub-genre of word-play is not unknown in Indonesia (e.g., see Pradopo, Widati, Maharto, Hariyono, & Faruk 1987: 130-134; and Dananandjaja 1988: 31); the concept is described using the English word "pun", not the Indonesian word *pun* which has an unrelated meaning.[2] Puns generally rely upon using

---

[2]Redfern (1984: 164; personal communication) intentionally misleads in explaining the pun in Malay, thus punning.

a homophonic connection between two or more meanings from a single word or phrase, resulting in a joke. Redfern (1984: 82) more broadly defines it as the "figurative use of a word or phrase." While the pun usually exists in a transient folkloric level such as joke telling, it also can also be revelatory of psychological dysfunction. For example, Abraham (1927: 363) reported that one of his patients often read the German *fruchtbar* ("fruitful") as *furchtbar* ("frightful") which was interpreted as being a symptom of the patient's dysfunction. This transformation is also illustrative of some of the overlap between puns and ludlings, since it also falls into the ludling class of transformations. There are relatively few words in Prokem that fall into both the category pun and the category ludling; Table 7 reports these.

Despite the difficulty of translating such an abstract idea as the pun between languages, it seems clear that many words and phrases in Prokem are puns. That is, they are puns because they either 1) have two meanings, one standard and one humorous or 2) they have a definition that sounds similar but means something different. In Prokem, puns are 1) acronymic redefinitions of acronyms (e.g., *APIK*, whose Indonesian definition is *Akademi Pendidikan Ilmu Keguruan* ["Training Academy of Science Teachers"], is redefined in Prokem as *agak pikun* ["rather senile"]) or 2) acronymic redefinitions of regular words (e.g., *ANGGUN*, "well dressed", is redefined in Prokem as *angota ragunan*, "ugly person", literally "member of the Ragunan Zoo in

Jakarta"), and 3) simple redefinitions (e.g. *anak mami*, "mama's child" or "child of a whorehouse madam" is redefined as *anak manja*, "spoiled child" [Rahardja and Chambert-Loir 1990: 40]).

The use of puns has a long history in Indonesia. *Sĕrat Cĕnthini*, a Javanese book from the early 1800s, frequently had alliterations and puns (Anderson 1990: 127, 295). For example, the double meaning of *klètèt*, "opium-ball" and "turd", was exploited in this book (Anderson 1990: 295). This same analogy is also found in Prokem (*be'o* and *cik*) as well as in English (e.g., see Partridge 1984: 1052-1053).

Religious punning is also found in Java, specifically in the *wayang* (shadow-puppet play) called *Kalimasada*. "The riddling pun is of great importance to the Javanese Islamic tradition, since it represents a sort of "capsulated intuition." (Anderson 1990: 127-128) The Prokem phrase, *air Zamzam*, meaning *bir* ("beer") is an example of a religious pun, but a blasphemous one. The name of the sacred well in Mecca is *Bîr Zamzam*, and *air Zamzam* is water from this well. The word *bîr* is from the Arabic for "well", and *bir* is from the Dutch *bier* ("beer"). Blasphemy does not necessarily indicate anti-religious sentiment, but more often indicates profound religiosity (Legman 1975: 760; Hughes 1991: 55-56). Blasphemy is most commonly found in highly religious societies (e.g., see Averna and Salemi 1982) and acts as an "escape valve" from religious domination (Legman 1975: 760).

Beginning with the Sukarno era, the widespread use of political acronyms had the effect of burying concepts into non-functional words (e.g. *JAREK* meant "*Jalan Revolusi Kita* (the Path of Our Revolution)", *RESOPIM* meant "*Revolusi-Sosialisme-Pimpinan* (Revolution-Socialism-Leadership)", and *USDEK* meant "*Undang-undang Dasar 1945, Socialisme à la Indonesia, Demokrasi Terpimpin, Ekonomi Terpimpin, Kepribadian Nasional* (the 1945 Constitution, Indonesian Socialism, Guided Democracy, Guided Economy, and National Identity)." (Anderson 1990: 147) Some Indonesian words have had their meanings reversed due to the transition from the "hopeful years of the revolution to the years that followed." (Anderson 1990: 141) The proliferation of acronyms beginning with the Sukarno era was probably most responsible for the large number of acronyms in Prokem.

"Punning appeals particularly to exiles (whether external or inner) for, having two homes and languages, the exile has a binary, split perspective (or strabismus) on his adopted culture." (Redfern 1984: 164) The multilingual and multicultural nature of Indonesia makes all of its population exiles within their own country in a sense, and it creates a predisposition for punning (since the majority of Indonesians speak more than one language, usually Indonesian and a local language). For Jakartans, the position of psychological exile is especially intense. First, there is a large population of domestic immigrants. Second, Jakarta is a linguistic island of sorts: Indonesian is the lingua franca of Indonesia and the principal language of Jakarta; additionally, Jakarta is surrounded by the traditional areas of Javanese and Sundanese speakers.

The duality of puns makes for appropriate verbal weapons under political or social repression. Because puns say two things at once, they can be directed to mean one thing to the oppressor and another to the oppressed (Redfern 1984: 124-125).

Despite popular notions, humor is often not a "laughing matter" (e.g., see Legman 1968; 1975), but rather an expression of the "belligerence of the insecure" (Redfern 1984: 123). As with most humor, punning has a strongly aggressive element (Freud 1960: 114-116; Redfern 1984: 108,123). Punning can also be characteristic of psychological disorder, such as persecution-mania (Redfern 1984: 103-110), as well as a psychological defense against real persecution, such as from a dictator or from law enforcement (Redfern 1984: 124-125).

To some Western observers, Indonesians may appear to use laughter in a wider range of emotions than themselves, representing "nervousness, fright, embarrassment, apology, anger, or sadness" (Draine & Hall 1986: 278). But this is overstated, since (nervous) laughter is a generalized expression of tension in humans (Legman 1975: 7-10). Laughter in humans is most likely derived from the facial expressions for fear and anger (Chevalier-Skolnikoff 1973: 26-28; Wilson 1975: 227-228; Apte 1985: 259). While fear and anger are probably universal antecedents of laughter, laughter and smiling are not universal expressions of joy (Apte 1985: 256-260). So, laughter among Westerners probably occurs for a similar range of emotions as Indonesians, though perhaps with different frequencies.

5. Crime

Partridge (1950a: 107; 1950b: Forward) believed that cant (criminal slang) was etymologically conservative compared to non-criminal slang. He believed that criminals are "slow to perceive that a word has become familiar to detectives, even to journalists, and therefore dangerous." (Partridge 1950a: 107) Hughes (1991: 138) notes that it is unusual for slang or colloquial terms to survive for over a century, but that a few have survived "four centuries without the support of respectability" and have entered common speech (Hughes 1988: 106). Legman (1964: 291) believes that slang can be divided into fake (short-lived), such as developed by commercial entertainment, and real (long-lived), as developed by "the folk." There is reason to believe that ludlings can be long lived as well: the one described by Ersine in 1933 is still used today in the United States and dates back to at least the 1770s (Ersine 1933; Wentworth & Flexner, 1975: 607-608). English Back Slang (similar to {Rp} in Table 2), has also been used among criminals since before 1850 (Beale 1989: 522). Except for a few archaisms, Pig Latin is probably not used by criminals, as it initially was (Ersine 1933; Wentworth and Flexner 1975: 648); it is today used by children.

The distinctions between real and artificial (or fake) slang are sometimes difficult to make. A Prokem speaker told me that some words that are considered by some to be Prokem were actually created by professional comedians. For example according to him, *SIMPATIK* (whose standard meaning is "congenial" or "sympathetic", and whose Prokem meaning is *simpanse pakai batik* ["chimpanzee dressed in batik"]) was created by the *Warung Kopi Prambors* comedy troupe, but later put into general use among the youth. Such transmission occurs in English as well, and goes in both directions. Such words are therefore in a gray-area of material that goes between folk- and commercial-lore. An example in U.S. slang is the use of the retort "Not!" to indicate that the previous statement was sarcastic. This was in use in the U.S. well before 1989 (Munro 1989: 139; Scheidlower & Lighter 1993), but subsequently re-popularized by professional comedians Dana Carvey and Mike Myers (from the U.S. television show "Saturday Night Live" and the 1992 movie "Wayne's World"), and brought into wider folk use. (See also Wentworth & Flexner [1975: 604-605] for a discussion of "artificial slang.") A related problem is that different subgroupings of a population will not always recognize words used by other subgroupings. For example, in U.S. slang, alcoholics often do not recognize words used by heroin users (Haertzen, Eisenberg, Hooks, Ross, & Pross 1979).

In English, one of the greatest expansions of swearing occurred during a period of great social repression: the Victorian era (Hughes 1991: 161). Rahardja and Chambert-Loir (1990: 86-87) stated that the spread of Prokem might be due to youthful cynicism and/or solidarity. Since Prokem contains a large number of words relating to topics such as sexuality, illegal drugs, crime and political corruption, it seems likely that repression has also been responsible for the growth of Prokem.

The period of Prokem's widespread student use corresponds both with standardization of Indonesian (e.g., see Osman 1986) and with the modern period (i.e., since 1957) of political and literary censorship[3] (Cribb 1992: 74-75). Repression of one form or another has probably existed for most of Indonesia's history (Ricklefs 1993: 17, 20), dating back at least as far as the brutal depopulation of Banda Island by the Dutch East India Company in the 1620s (Ricklefs 1993: 29-30). Press censorship has existed continuously and vigorously since 1856 with the exception of the revolutionary

---

[3]For example, Abeyasekere (1989), Dalton (1988; 1991), numerous news publications, and the writings of Mochtar Lubis (one of Indonesia's best writers) and other writers have been censored or banned (Dalton 1988: 1034; 1991: 18-19, 1051; Ricklefs 1993: 297, 300).

period of 1945-1949 (Thoolen 1987: 96-116; U.S. Department of State 1993: 573). From the time of independence until 1957, when martial law was declared, there was "virtually no political imprisonment." (Amnesty International 1977: 12-13) An abortive coup in 1965 led to the replacement of President Sukarno with then-General Suharto who remained president until 1998. Hundreds of thousands of people were summarily executed during the wake of the abortive coup. The modern Indonesian era ("The New Order") of political repression was initiated with tens of thousands becoming political prisoners. Political repression has continued past the period of the abortive coup. "The list of those detained... includes some of the most respected lawyers, academics, editors and poets in the country. Scores of students have been detained, as have a great many lower-level Muslim party officials." (Jenkins 1979; see also Ricklefs 1993: 296, 300, 306-307) Student organizations were relatively unthreatened by the government until the demonstrations of 1973-1974 that culminated in the Malari Affair (Thoolen 1987: 86,137-138). Notably, Chambert-Loir (1984: 115) stated that the widespread use among Jakartan students occurred primarily during the period 1970-1975.

In the United States, the Harrison Act of 1914 made many drugs illegal and consequently created a subculture with its own secret terminology (Maurer & High 1980: 185-186; Maurer 1981: 83-110). Similarly, since ganja (*Cannabis* spp.) was legal in Indonesia until 1927 (Cribb 1992: 71), it is unlikely that the numerous ganja-related terms (approximately 70) in Prokem came into existence until after then.

According to Abeyasekere (1989: 194), youth gangs appeared in Jakarta in the 1950s. "Some viewed them suspiciously as a sign of imported social decadence, but they also had much in common with the *pemuda* [youth] of the Revolution days." (Abeyasekere 1987: 194) But, gangsterism has existed in Java for centuries (Abeyasekere 1989: 172-173; Cribb 1991: 1; Cribb 1992: 42-43), just as sea piracy has flourished in the archipelago for centuries and continues to exist to this day (Cribb 1992: 42). Despite their efforts, the European colonial powers were unable to eradicate piracy in the 19th century. Piracy was considered to be "an honorable profession which was connived at, promoted, or even directly engaged in by the highest potentates." (Hall 1981: 568-569) For example, during the 18th century, the Bugis were noted both as merchants and as pirates (Hall 1981: 569).

The commingling of students and criminals may have begun during the revolutionary era after World War II when both groups were involved in the revolution (Cribb 1991: 57-67). After the revolution, however, criminals lost their legitimacy and either took "up their old criminal pursuits in their home territories or [moved] on to new occupations, criminal or otherwise, in Jakarta." (Cribb 1991: 183) Rural banditry was widespread during the period of chaos following independence, ending about 1956. But by the time of The New Order, rural banditry had become minimal while urban crimebecame rampant (Cribb 1992: 42-43). As in the U.S., students and criminals have also interacted since the 1960s in the area of illegal drug use. Finally, the Malari Affair of 1973-1974 drove student organizations underground.

Tables 8 and 9 list words that were in use during or prior to the revolution and are still in use in Prokem. The word *jago* (Table 8) was used in colonial Java to refer to rural opportunists who functioned primarily as thugs, but also as power brokers, anti-colonial forces, and land owners (Onghokham 1984: 327-328,339-340).

Table 9 lists those words associated with rural activity. During parts of the colonial Dutch period, gangs operated in the lands around Jakarta which were rural and not under strict control by either the Dutch or by traditional society, since these lands were near the Javanese and Sundanese cultural regions (Cribb 1991: 18-19, 28-29). This situation was different than for the criminals of Jakarta today who probably operate principally within urban areas. However, there has always been rural migration to Jakarta, and Jakarta remains relatively near farming areas, so the linguistic association of these words is at best a weak indication of an origin in rural banditry.

Corruption is widespread in Indonesia, and while nominally illegal, it is rarely acted against (Dalton 1991: 26-27; see also Ricklefs 1993). Prokem speakers who encounter corruption are more likely to be on the losing end since it is bureaucrats and corporations who are most likely to benefit from corruption. Hence, one expects and finds that terms in Prokem relating to corruption would be different than other crime-related terms. Eight percent (2/25) of corruption terms use euphemism or pun {O} vs. 51% (155/302) of other criminal terms (χ^2 p<0.0001); 62% (28/45) of corruption terms use multiple transformations vs. 27% (92/335) of other criminal terms (χ^2 p<0.0001); and 48% (12/25) of corruption terms are acronyms vs. 10% (33/328) of other terms (χ^2 p<0.0001). Consequently, terms relating to corruption are removed from the following analyses, since they are both functionally and statistically different than other criminal subcategories.

Prostitution is partly legalized in Indonesia, but the legality applies only to regulated complexes and not to the large numbers of women who do not work in them; prostitution is stigmatized both socially and by police raids (Murray 1991: 84, 105-106). Furthermore, prostitutes frequently are users of illegal drugs (Murray 1991: 103-104). Hence the language of prostitutes would be expected to resemble activities that are completely illegal. Forty-four percent (17/39) of prostitution words are formed by the {O} transformation, compared to 52% of other criminal words (137/262, χ^2 p=0.3). There is also no difference between prostitution terms and other criminal terms with regard to multiple transformations: 22% (10/45) are multiple transformations vs. 28% (81/288) of other criminal terms (χ^2 p=0.4). There is however a difference between prostitution terms and other criminal terms for acronyms: 31% (13/42) of prostitution terms are acronyms vs. 7% of other criminal terms (20/285, χ^2 $p<0.0001$). These results are similar for the data from Rahardja and Chambert-Loir, except that there is a slight difference between prostitution and other crime terms for the {O} transformation: 43% (13/30) vs. 62% (104/167, χ^2 $p=0.05$). Since there is some difference between prostitution and other criminal terms, but the functionalities are similar, the analyses below were done both with and without prostitution terms, but the results did not change with the exclusion of prostitution terms.

About 25% of all Prokem meanings are crime-related. Criminal subcategories and the percentages of their occurrence relative to all Prokem meanings are: barbiturates (2%), ganja (6%), opiates (2%), other or unspecified drugs (1%), theft (3%), and prostitution (3%); the remaining 8% of crime-related meanings are general. Political corruption (not included in the analyses below) occurs in about 3% of all Prokem meanings.

Crime-related words are more often formed by euphemism or pun {O} than are other words: 48% (154/301) vs. 22% (289/1291), χ^2 $p<0.0001$.

Criminal categories are less often formed from multiple transformations than other categories: 27% (91/333) vs. 45% (627/1404), χ^2 $p<0.0001$. This also holds true for the criminal subcategories other than political corruption, and for Rahardja and Chambert-Loir (1988; 1990) data except for the theft subcategory.

The theft subcategory is less often formed from multiple transformations than other non-criminal categories, but this is not true for the Rahardja and Chambert-Loir data alone for which the percentages are each about 40%.

Acronyms are equally common for criminal words as for non-criminal words: 10% (33/294) vs. 10% (127/1317). This holds true for the criminal subcategories and for the data from Rahardja and Chambert-Loir.

6. Sex and Violence

Folklore can reveal a truth that remains hidden because it is embarrassing, such as the existence of torture in Indonesia which has in the past been officially denied or minimized by the government (Amnesty International 1977: 71-76; U.S. Department of State 1993: 570-571), but which is irrefutably revealed by the existence of words for it in Prokem (see Table 10).

In comparing sex and violence it is instructive to examine film, since these subjects are often juxtaposed there. There are six words for pornographic film (Table 11), none of whose meanings would be obvious to a non-Prokem speaking Indonesian. In contrast, Prokem only contains three words for film in general (Table 11). To someone who knows a little about Prokem, these three words are easier to guess, since two are ludic transformations (*lepem* and *lipem*) and the third is an obvious euphemism (*sorot*). Pornographic films are illegal in Indonesia, and all films are subject to official censorship, particularly for political and sexual matter (Heider 1991: 22-23). "Sexuality is one of the most sensitive subjects in Indonesian life." (Heider 1991: 66) Censorship of Indonesian films represents the most conservative and hence least offensive cultural norms of Indonesia, typically Javanese (Heider 1991: 68), the dominant Indonesian culture. Censorship in Indonesia is overtly inconsistent because different norms are used for censorship of domestically produced films than are used for widely available imported films (Heider 1991: 66). For example, until recently "full lip-to-lip kisses" have been banned from domestic films; heterosexual, palm-to-palm hand holding (which is more taboo than full kisses) continues to be banned in domestically produced film (Heider 1991: 67). Nudity has been permitted in Indonesian-made films but only in the context of rape or other sadistic sex (Heider 1991: 41-42). Censorship is also covertly inconsistent, at least in Jakarta, since despite being illegal, 73% of 13-23 year old Jakartans polled (N=417) viewed pornographic materials (films or printed matter) at least once (Sarwono 1981: 9-10,24). It is notable that this is also approximately the primary age of non-pornographic movie theater attendees: ages 15-24 (Heider 1991: 21), and is within the age range of Prokem speakers (elementary to university level students [Chambert-Loir 1984: 116]).

It is not surprising that depiction of sexuality is censored in Indonesia, but that depiction of violence is not. Though Indonesia is a secular state, Islam is the dominant religion and consequently is an important influence on national consensus. Globally, censorship of sex is probably more prevalent than censorship of violence, for example sex is the primary indicator in the United States' Motion Picture Association of America rating system. Violence or sadism often substitutes for sex in folklore and literature, particularly when there is censorship (Legman 1949; 1964: 306-308; 1968; 1975). Violence and sex are probably linked for ethological reasons (e.g., see Lorenz 1966: 117-124; La Barre 1970: 170; Eysenck and Nias 1978: 171-176,247-250). It is likely that the viewing of violence encourages patriotism (e.g. see Keen 1986; and Lester, Hudson, & Costic 1992). In contrast, sexuality has often been the subject of censorship during times of political oppression (Legman 1949; 1964; Tannahill 1980). In recent times, this may be due to the association of anti-communism with religion and "family values", hence an erroneous association of communism with sexual liberalism (e.g., see Heider 1991: 72). Whereas the Indonesian government acknowledged a rise in acts of sexual violence, it associated it with rapid urbanization (U.S. Department of State 1993: 577) rather than with the culture of official violence, which was the more obvious cause.

Japan shares with Indonesia an emphasis on social order and conformity (Heider 1991: 34-38; Sabin 1993: 208). Japanese comics, which are extremely popular in Japan, often depict graphic violence, and often only depict sex in the context of sadism; these "themes are tolerated because Japanese officialdom sees fictional violence, sexual or otherwise, as a safety valve." (Sabin 1993: 208) Such is probably also the case in Indonesia. The viewing of violence desensitizes oneself towards violence (Eysenck & Nias 1978: 55-56,180-184), but this does not necessarily mean that it causes real violence (Eysenck & Nias 1978: 204-205; Cumberbatch 1989). For example, Japan and Indonesia have widespread access to fictional depictions of violence, but have low levels of violent crime (Kidron & Segal 1984: 44; Sabin 1993: 208).

About 15% of all Prokem meanings are sex-related, and about 5% of meanings are violence-related. Sex-related subcategories and their percentages of occurrence relative to all Prokem meanings are: prostitution (3%), homosexuality (1%), and transvestitism/transsexualism (1%); the remaining 10% of sex-related meanings are general.

Considering all data, there is no difference between sex categories and the violence category with regard to use of euphemism or pun {O}. Thirty-five percent (86/245) of the sex categories use euphemism or pun vs. 39% (26/67) of violence-related words (χ^2 p=0.6). There is also no difference when the sex categories are analyzed separately. After excluding data only from Rahardja and Chambert-Loir (1988; 1990), there is some difference: 39% (63/163) for sex-related terms vs. 57% (21/37, χ^2 p=0.04) for the violence category. However, in comparing the sex subcategories individually against the violence category for the

Rahardja and Chambert-Loir data, no difference is found, hence this is a dubious result.

There is no difference between sex and violence categories as to whether multiple transformations have been used: 34% (96/281) vs. 32% (22/68). Sex subcategories are also similar as well as data from Rahardja and Chambert-Loir alone.

There is however a difference between sex and violence with regard to acronyms; 21% (53/254) of sex categories are based on acronyms {_} vs. only 6% (4/67) of violence categories (χ^2 p=0.005). This also holds true for the sex subgroups, and for Rahardja and Chambert-Loir data alone.

.

Discussion

There is no difference between sex and violence for euphemism, pun or multiple transformation; this does not necessarily contradict other information. The lack of difference may reflect interpersonal relations rather than other arenas such as film or the military where violence is clearly less taboo. The acronym {_} is often used in a joking manner to form riddles (Indonesian, *teka-teki*). This could explain why there is a difference between sex and violence for acronyms but not for the other obscuring mechanisms. In other words, while euphemism, pun and multiple transformations may act to obscure for secrecy, the obscurity of the acronym is utilized as the fulcrum of a joke. Sex is a frequent topic of humor, whereas violence (without sex) is rarely so. This is reflected by large compendia of sex-related humor in English (e.g., Legman 1968; 1975), and a modest compendium in Indonesian (Danandjaja 1988). Violent (or aggressive) humor in English is typically directed at a social subgroup such as women or ethnic minorities (Dundes 1987) and is hence not strictly about violence but about xenophobia.

Words relating to criminal activities are more obscure than other words; this is not surprising since being caught at criminal activity carries a very real punishment not associated with other Prokem topics. The weak difference for acronyms is again suggestive that the acronym functions more often for humor than for purposes of secrecy. Criminal categories are less often multiple transformations; this indicates that multiple transformations may not be a good measure of obscurity. About half of all multiple transformations are $\{ok_1+C\}$ or $\{ok_2+C\}$ and hence not particularly more obscure then $\{ok_1\}$ or $\{ok_2\}$ alone. Furthermore, it is not possible to statistically analyze these subjects for single vs. multiple transformations after removing those with $\{ok_1\}$ or $\{ok_2\}$, since very few non-$\{ok_x\}$ multiple transformations occur in the crime (N=3), sex (N=2), or violence (N=0) categories.

There is little evidence to support the idea that Prokem came from external sources any more than other influences on language in Jakarta. Etymological evidence from other languages is minor, and sociolinguistic evidence indicates that external sources are unlikely to have had a greater influence on Prokem than on other aspects of Jakartan life. The existence of other ludlings in Indonesia and Malaysia with similarities to Prokem does not necessarily indicate an external source either, since these ludlings may have arisen independently or may have all had a common ancestor. Though there is a surprising correspondence between Cakap Balik and Prokem, the majority of the small vocabulary reported for Cakap Balik has not been reported in Prokem (46/54, 85%).

Prokem exists as one of several linguistic codes (i.e. language subsets that indicate the status of the speaker) within the Jakartan dialect of Indonesian (Grijns 1991) as well as within the Javanese and Sundanese substrata and within other languages in Indonesia (Wolff & Poedjosoedarmo 1982: 8). That Prokem exists in the form that it does in the place that it does is not surprising. Jakarta is Indonesia's linguistic and ethnic crossroads, and as such it potentially has contact with ludlings and other languages from throughout the archipelago. This could explain the complexity of Prokem. Criminals and the political elite had opportunistic contact during the revolutionary era, and hence cant (or criminal slang) was probably part of Prokem at least as early as the 1940s (Cribb 1991: 57-67), and was probably reinfused since the 1960s by student drug use. Political repression of intellectuals has been persistent both in modern and colonial Indonesia (and more recently of students specifically), and hence there has been a consistent need for a secretive language among the educated, in addition to the more common existence of a cant.

A parallel to this situation exists in English: Pig Latin was originally used by criminals (Ersine 1933: 10). That Prokem seems to have had an origin in the underworld is not surprising given that the earliest records of slang from England, France, Germany, Italy and Spain are of thieves' slang (Partridge 1934: 41-42). Another more specific parallel is that there was a large infusion of drug slang into youth speech in the U.S. (Wentworth & Flexner 1975: 670).

1. Other Polysystemic Slangs Outside Malaysia and Indonesia

The French code language called Verlan (Lefkowitz 1991) is probably the best parallel to Prokem. Like Prokem, it includes words relating to crime and drugs (Lefkowitz 1991: 64, 66, 117), it is strongly ludic but not predictably so (Lefkowitz 1991: 26-28, 71-104), it is used by both students and criminals (Paul 1985: 38; Lefkowitz 1991: 58-59, 64), and its use is anti-authoritarian (Lefkowitz 1991: 65). Verlan differs from Prokem in that its modern popularization has been by minorities, particularly second-generation north Africans in the Parisian suburbs (Lefkowitz 1991: 54-55) although it dates to the 19th century or earlier when it was a cant (Lefkowitz 1991: 50-53).

Notably, there are English words not only in Prokem, but also in Verlan (Lefkowitz 1991). This is probably not only due to the worldwide prevalence of English, but also due to knowledge of English as a secondary language being a status symbol.

Why is it that polysystemic languages exist based on French and Indonesian, but not apparently purely based on English? French and English speaking countries have had many ludlings (Laycock 1972: 103), and so has Indonesia (Simons 1982). "Three cultural conditions especially contribute to the creation of a large slang vocabulary: 1) hospitality to or acceptance of new objects, situations, and concepts; 2) existence of a large number of diversified sub-groups; 3) democratic mingling between these sub-groups and the dominant culture." (Wentworth & Flexner 1975: x) These conditions exist in America, Australia, Britain, and Canada, so the difference is not explained by these conditions, particularly since English has a large slang vocabulary (but with only a minor ludic element). The difference could be explained by the multi-lingual nature of Indonesia and the large Arabic speaking population in and around Paris. However, this still does not completely explain the apparent lack of a polysystemic ludling in English-speaking countries since there are bilingual communities in these countries.

2. Prokem in the Larger Slang Context

Slang is a radical form of speech since it often operates under fewer social constraints than normal language (Partridge 1934: 35). Language transformation, too, is often radical. There is great attachment to Indonesian as the national language of Indonesia: an early nationalist slogan was: "One Nation, One Country, One Language!" (*Satu Tanah Air, Satu Bangsa, Satu Bahasa!*) [Dalton 1991: 31]. This slogan was parodied in the Indonesian newspaper, *Kompas* (October 28, 1981) and reprinted in Rahardja and Chambert-Loir (1988; 1990: viii). The parody used Dutch, Indonesian and Prokem, and hence illustrated the partial illusion of Indonesian as the national language: on the one hand, one can go anywhere in

Indonesia and speak Indonesian, but on the other, one can go anywhere and hear other languages as well.

Any large population will consist of sub-groupings with their own vocabularies; these subgroupings will overlap somewhat (Wentworth & Flexner 1975: vi-viii; see also Haertzen et al. 1979). Consequently, it is some-times difficult to decide whether a slang be-longs to a particular subgroup. Prokem is not the only slang spoken in Jakarta, and it has re-ceived some words from other slangs (e.g., the Bencong slang of transvestites and transsexu-als; Table 5). Probable subgroupings that have contributed to Prokem are: transves-tites / transsexuals, homosexuals (though not from their own slang), prostitutes, street gangs (*preman*), criminals, high school students, and college students. These subgroupings are similar to the ones described by Wentworth and Flexner (1975: vii) for English except that professional subgroupings such as musicians appear to be better represented in English slang.

Negation of the original meaning of a word is a common process in slang (Wentworth & Flexner 1975: xi-xii). The process of nega-tion is a symptomatic reaction of an oppressed minority within a society, e.g. African-Ameri-cans have used a process that Sims Holt (1972) calls "inversion": the exaggeration of labels for insult (e.g., calling a white army corporal a "captain") or for solidarity (e.g., African-American use of "nigger" in some circum-stances). This process has also been used in

Jamaican Creole, and has often been unrecognized or misunderstood (Sims Holt 1972: 158; Campbell 1987: 22, 99). Negation of meaning is found frequently in Prokem under the {O} transformation, e.g. *gol* (meaning "goal" in Indonesian, and "to enter prison" in Prokem). This process indicates the oppression of the criminal element by law enforcement, but also of the student element by reduced expectations from high unemployment, from government repression, from widespread corruption and from the undiscussible (e.g., the events that led up to The New Order). These have at least until recently been unresolved political events.

Conclusion

Prokem is a slang that is remarkably complex because it was formed from multiple methods, both ludic and non-ludic. The complexity indicates that it is not entirely of recent invention. There is some evidence that Cakap Balik, a slang from Negri Sembilan State in Malaysia, has an ancestral relationship to Prokem, but the data is limited. There is even less evidence of an origin in Sumatra. Lacking any evidence to the contrary, it is reasonable to believe that most of the development of Prokem occurred in Jakarta where it is exclusively spoken.

There is good reason to believe that Prokem was originally a criminal language (or cant). Numerous crime-related words exist in current Prokem, and several words in Prokem indicate an origin in rural banditry. Several events are likely to have provided opportunistic transference of Prokem from criminal to wider usage: contact between criminals and revolutionaries prior to Indonesian independence, imprisonment of intellectuals and other political imprisonment beginning with the New Order, students' illicit drug use primarily beginning in the 1960s, and the Malari Affair of the early 1970s that drove certain student groups underground.

The secrecy of Prokem enables its speakers to more readily talk about taboo topics. Both sex and violence have taboo values in Indonesian society, but depiction of violence (especially in film) is more readily accepted. A greater percentage of Prokem words are sex-related (15%) than are violence-related (5%). Sex-related words are more often part of acronyms than are violence-related words (21% vs. 6%); since acronyms are often used in riddles (*teka-teki*) in Indonesia, this suggests that humor is being used as a psychological release for sex taboos more so than violence taboos. However, euphemisms, which also may be humorous though less overtly, are equally likely to be used for sex or violence.

Though corruption has been discussed openly and in the Indonesian press, generally little action has been taken against it. Many Prokem terms dealing with corruption are acronyms, suggesting that there is substantial frustration with corruption and that the psychological release of humor is one way that Prokem speakers deal with it.

References

Abeyasekere, Susan (1989). *Jakarta: A History*. New York: Oxford University Press, 2nd edition.

Abraham, Karl (1927). *Selected Papers on Psychoanalysis*. Translated by Douglas Bryan and Alix Strachey. New York: Basic Books.

Allan, Keith and Kate Burridge (1991). *Euphemism and Dysphemism: Language Used as Shield and Weapon*. New York: Oxford University Press.

Amien, Raisha. *Kamus Bahasa Kawula Muda*. Jakarta: Pustaka Bintang, 1988.

Amnesty International (1977). *Indonesia: An Amnesty International Report*. London: Amnesty International Publications.

Anderson, Benedict R. O'Gorman (1990). *Language and Power: Exploring Political Cultures in Indonesia*. Ithaca: Cornell University Press.

Apte, Mahadev L. (1985). *Humor and Laughter: An Anthropological Approach*. Ithaca, New York: Cornell University Press.

Atmojo, Kemala (1986). *Kami Bukan Lelaki: Sebuah Sketsa Kehidupan Kaum Waria*. Jakarta: Grafiti Pers.

Averna, Giuliano and Joseph Salemi (1982). "Italian blasphemies." *Maledicta: The International Journal of Verbal Aggression* 6: 63-70.

Beale, Paul, ed. (1989). *Partridge's Concise Dictionary of Slang and Unconventional English; From a Dictionary of Slang and Unconventional English by Eric Partridge*. New York: Macmillan.

Brunvand, Jan Harold (1968). *The Study of American Folklore: An Introduction*. New York: W.W. Norton.

Campbell, Horace (1987). *Rasta and Resistance: From Marcus Garvey to Walter Rodney*. Trenton, New Jersey: Africa World Press.

Castles, Lance (1967). "The ethnic profile of Djakarta." *Indonesia* 3: 153-204.

Chambert-Loir, Henri (1983). "Mereka yang berbahasa Prokem." In *Citra Masyarakat Indonesia*, 112-130. Jakarta: Sinar Harapan/ Archipel.

— (1983). "Those who speak Prokem." *Indonesia* 37 (1984): 105-117. Translated by James T. Collins from Chambert-Loir.

— (1990). "Prokem, the slang of Jakarta youth: Instructions for use." *Prisma: The Indonesian Indicator* 50: 80-88. [This is an English translation of Rahardja and Chambert-Loir (1988: 1-17), which is reprinted in Rahardja and Chambert-Loir (1990: 1-24). Citations are given for the English language reference throughout the text even though they apply to all 3 references.]

Chapman, Robert L., ed. (1986). *New Dictionary of American Slang*. New York: Harper and Row. [Revised edition of Wentworth and Flexner (1975)]

Chevalier-Skolnikoff, Suzanne (1973). "Facial expression of emotion in nonhuman primates." In *Darwin and Facial Expression: A Century of Research in Review*, edited by Paul Ekman,11-89. New York: Academic Press.

Chomsky, Noam and Morris Halle (1968). *The Sound Pattern of English*. New York: Harper and Row.

Cralle, Trevor (1991). *The Surfin'ary: A Dictionary of Surfing Terms and Surfspeak*. Berkeley, California: Ten Speed Press.

Cribb, Robert (1991). *Gangsters and Revolutionaries: The Jakarta People's Militia and the Indonesian Revolution 1945-1949*. Honolulu: University of Hawaii Press.

Cribb, Robert (1992). *Historical Dictionary of Indonesia*. Asian Historical Dictionaries no. 9. Metuchen, New Jersey: Scarecrow Press.

Cumberbatch, Guy (1989). "Violence and the mass media: The research evidence." In *A Measure of Uncertainty: The Effects of the Mass Media*, edited by Guy Cumberbatch and Dennis Howitt, 31-59. London: John Libbey.

Dalton, Bill (1991). *Indonesia Handbook*. Chico, California: Moon Publications, 5th edition.

Danandjaja, James (1988). *Humor Mahasiswa Jakarta. Buku 1: Lelucon Erotik*. Jakarta: Sinar Harapan.

De Josselin De Jong, Patrick Edward (1922). *Minangkabau and Negri Sembilan: Socio-Political Structure in Indonesia.* Leiden, Netherlands: Eduard Ijdo.

Di Lauro, Al and Rabkin, Gerald (1976). *Dirty Movies: An Illustrated History of the Stag Film 1915-1970.* New York: Chelsea House.

Draine, Cathie and Barbara Hall (1986). *Culture Shock! Indonesia.* Singapore: Times Books International.

Dreyfuss, J. (1983). "The backward language of Jakarta youth: A bird of many language feathers." *Nusa* 16: 52-56.

Dundes, Alan (1980). *Interpreting Folklore.* Bloomington: Indiana University Press.

Dundes, Alan (1987). *Cracking Jokes: Studies of Sick Humor Cycles and Stereotypes.* Berkeley, California: Ten Speed Press.

Dundes, Alan and Carl R. Pagter (1987). *When You're Up to Your Ass in Alligators... More Urban Folklore from the Paperwork Empire.* Detroit, Michigan: Wayne State University Press.

Ersine, Noel (1933). *Underworld and Prison Slang.* Upland, Indiana: A. D. Freese and Son.

Evans, Ivor Hugh Norman (1917). "Malay back-slang." *Journal of the Federated Malay States Museums* 7: 115-116.

Evans, Ivor Hugh Norman (1923). *Studies in Religion, Folk-Lore and Custom in British North Borneo and the Malay Peninsula.* Cambridge: University Press.

Eysenck, H. J. and D. K. B. Nias (1978). *Sex, Violence and the Media.* New York: St. Martin's Press.

Foley, W. A. (1983a). "Sumatra." In *Language Atlas of the Pacific Area. Part II. Japan Area, Taiwan (Formosa), Philippines, Mainland and Insular South-East Asia,* edited by S. A. Wurm and Shirô Hattori. Canberra: Australian National University. Pacific Linguistics Series C-67.

Foley, W. A. (1983b). "Java and Bali." In *Language Atlas of the Pacific Area. Part II. Japan Area, Taiwan (Formosa), Philippines, Mainland and Insular South-East Asia,* edited by S. A. Wurm and Shirô Hattori. Canberra: Australian National University. Pacific Linguistics Series C-67.

Freud, Sigmund (1960). *Jokes and Their Relation to the Unconscious.* Translated by James Strachey. New York: W. W. Norton (paperback edition 1989).

Gandour, Jackson T. (1978). "Talking backwards about sex (etc.) in Thai." *Maledicta: The International Journal of Verbal Aggression* 2: 111-114.

Grijns, C. D. (1991). *Jakarta Malay: A Multidimensional Approach to Spatial Variation.* Vol. 1. Leiden, Netherlands: KITLV Press.

Gurdon, Meghan Cox (1992). "Malaysian law tries to regulate racism." *San Francisco Chronicle,* 3 July, p. A16.

Haertzen, Charles A., H. Allan Eisenberg, Nall T. Hooks Jr., Frances E. Ross and Mary Pross (1979). "Estimating specificity of drug and alcohol subcultural groups with slang names for drugs." *Journal of Consulting and Clinical Psychology* 47: 592-594.

Hall, Daniel George Edward (1981). *A History of South-East Asia*. New York: St. Martin's Press, 4th edition.

Heider, Karl G. (1991). *Indonesian Cinema: National Culture on Screen*. Honolulu: University of Hawaii Press.

Horne, Elinor Clark (1974). *A Javanese-English Dictionary*. New Haven, Connecticut: Yale University Press.

Hughes, Geoffrey (1988). *Words in Time: A Social History of the English Vocabulary*. Cambridge, Massachusetts: Basil Blackwell.

Hughes, Geoffrey (1991). *Swearing: A Social History of Foul Language, Oaths and Profanity in English*. Cambridge, Massachusetts: Basil Blackwell.

Jasawijata and Kartadarmadja (1921). "Eenige voorbelden van geheime taal in het Javaansch." *Djawa* 1, no. 3: 53-54.

Jenkins, David (1979). "Keeping the opposition in line." *Far Eastern Economic Review* 104, no. 17: 24.

Kasim, Nurlena Basier and Richard Sinaga (1989). *Kamus Pelajar: Istilah Ilmu Pengetahuan, Istilah Umum, Kata-kata Asing, Kata-kata Baru, Singkatan dalam Basahaku Bahasa Indonesia.* Jakarta: Angin Sejuk , 4th edition.

Keen, Sam (1986). *Faces of the Enemy: Reflections of the Hostile Imagination. The Psychology of Enmity.* New York: Harper and Row.

Kidron, Michael and Ronald Segal (1984). *The New State of the World Atlas.* New York: Simon and Schuster.

La Barre, Weston (1970). *The Ghost Dance: Origins of Religion.* Garden City, New York: Doubleday.

Laycock, Don (1972). "Towards a typology of ludlings, or play-languages." *Linguistic Communications: Working Papers of the Linguistic Society of Australia* 6: 61-113.

Lefkowitz, Natalie (1991). *Talking Backwards, Looking Forwards: The French Language Game Verlan.* Language in Performance No.3. Tübingen, Germany: Gunter Narr Verlag.

Legman, Gershon (1949). *Love and Death: A Study in Censorship.* New York: Breaking Point.

Legman, Gershon (1964).*The Horn Book: Studies in Erotic Folklore and Bibliography.* New Hyde Park, New York: University Books.

Legman, Gershon (1968). *Rationale of the Dirty Joke: An Analysis of Sexual Humor.* 1st Series. New York: Grove Press.

Legman, Gershon (1975). *No Laughing Matter: An Analysis of Sexual Humor.* 2nd Series. New York: Bell.

Lester, David, Robert B. Hudson, and Jean Costic (1992). "Arousing patriotic feelings in men and women." *Perceptual and Motor Skills* 75: 914.

Lorenz, Konrad (1966). *On Aggression*. New York: Harcourt, Brace and World. (1st paperback edition ,1967, Bantam Books, New York).

Lumintaintang, Yayah B. (1981). *Pemakaian Bahasa Indonesia dan Dialek Jakarta di SMA Jakarta*. Jakarta: Pusat Pembinaan dan Pengembangan Bahasa, Departemen Pendidikan dan Kebudayaan.

Malinowski, Bronislaw (1927). *Sex and Repression in Savage Society*. New York: Harcourt, Brace. (1st paperback edition, 1955, Meridian Books, New York).

Mardiwarsito, L., Sukesi Adiwimarta and Timur Suratman (1985). *Kamus Praktis Jawa-Indonesia*. Jakarta, Indonesia: Pusat Pembinaan dan Pengembangan Bahasa, Departemen Pendidikan dan Kebudayaan.

Maurer, David W. (1981). *Language of the Underworld*. Allan W. Futrell and Charles B. Wordell, eds. Lexington: University Press of Kentucky.

Maurer, David W. and Ellesa Clay High (1980). "New words — Where do they come from and where do they go? An Experiment in cavalier lexicography." *American Speech* 55: 184-194.

Mörzer Bruyns, A. (1970). *Kamus Singkatan dan Akronim jang Dipergunakan di Indonesia. Glossary of Abbreviations and Acronyms used in Indonesia.* Jakarta: Ichtiar.

Munro, Pamela (1989). *Slang U.* New York: Harmony Books.

Murray, Alison J. (1991). *No Money, No Honey: A Study of Street Traders and Prostitutes in Jakarta.* New York: Oxford University Press.

Naim, Mochtar (1974). *Merantau: Minangkabau Voluntary Migration.* Ph.D. dissertation, University of Singapore.

Nash, Jay Robert (1992). *Dictionary of Crime: Criminal Justice, Criminology, and Law Enforcement.* New York: Paragon House.

Oemarjati, Boen S. (1980). "Ragam Bahasa Remaja: Permainan kata tanpa batas." *Analisis Kebudayaan* 1(3): 62-70.

Onghokham (1984). "The *jago* in colonial Java, ambivalent champion of the people." In *History and Peasant Consciousness in South East Asia*, edited by Andrew Turton and Shigeharu Tanabe, 327-343. Senri Ethnological Studies No.13. Osaka, Japan: National Museum of Ethnology.

Osman, Mohamed Taib (1986). *An Introduction to the Development of Modern Malay Language and Literature.* Singapore: Times Books International, revised edition.

Partridge, Eric (1934). *Slang To-Day and Yesterday: With a Short Historical Sketch and Vocabularies of English, American and Australian Slang*. New York: Macmillan.

Partridge, Eric (1950a). *Here, There, and Everywhere: Essays upon Language*. London: Hamish Hamilton, 2nd edition.

Partridge, Eric (1950b). *A Dictionary of the Underworld*. London: Routledge and Kegan Paul (Hertfordshire, England: Wordsworth Editions, 1989).

Partridge, Eric (1984). *A Dictionary of Slang and Unconventional English: Colloquialisms and Catch-phrases, Solecisms and Catachreses, Nicknames and Vulgarisms*. Paul Beale, ed. New York: Macmillan, 8th edition.

Paul, Elizabeth (1985). *Etude des Regularités Morpho-syntaxiques du Verlan Contemporain*. Unpublished Mémoire de Maîtrise. Paris: U.E.R. de Linguistique Française. [cited in Lefkowitz (1991)].

Pelzer, Karl J. (1978). *Planter and Peasant: Colonial Policy and the Agrarian Struggle in East Sumatra, 1863-1947*. Verhandelingen van Het Kininklijk Instituut voor Taal-, Land- en Volkenkunde no.84. 'S-Gravenhage, Netherlands: Martinus Nijhoff.

Pradopo, Sri Widati, Siti Soendari Maharto, Ratna Indriani Hariyono and H. T. Faruk (1987). *Humor dalam Sastra Jawa Modern*. Jakarta: Pusat Pembinaan dan

Pengembangan Bahasa, Departemen Pendidikan dan Kebudayaan.

Prentice, D. J. (1982). "Some ludic aspects of Timugon Murut." In *Papers from the Third International Conference on Austronesian Linguistics.* Volume 3, edited by Amran Halim, Lois Carrington and Stephen A. Wurm. Canberra: Australian National University. Pacific Linguistics Series C-76, pp. 145-155.

Pukui, Mary Kawena, Samuel H. Elbert and Esther T. Mookini (1975). *The Pocket Hawaiian Dictionary With a Concise Hawaiian Grammar.* Honolulu: University of Hawaii Press.

Pur, Samuel Labo (1989). *Kamus Bahasa Khas Kawula Muda.* Jakarta: Generasi Harapan.

Rahman, Azizul Rahman Abdul (1995). *Bahasa Rahsia Bahasa Melayu.* Bangi: Universiti Kebangsaan Malaysia.

Rahardja, Prathama and Henri Chambert-Loir (1988). *Kamus Bahasa Prokem.* Jakarta: Grafiti Pers, 1st edition.

Rahardja, Prathama and Henri Chambert-Loir (1990). *Kamus Bahasa Prokem.* Jakarta: Utama Grafiti, 2nd edition.

Redfern, Walter (1984). *Puns.* New York: Basil Blackwell.

Ricklefs, M. C. (1993). *A History of Modern Indonesia since c. 1300.* Stanford, California: Stanford University Press, 2nd edition.

Sabin, Roger (1993). *Adult Comics: An Introduction.* New York: Routledge.

Sadtono, E. (1971). "Language games in Javanese." *Penn-Texas Working Papers in Sociolinguistics* 2: 32-38.

Sarwono, Sarlito Wirawan (1981). *Pergeseran Norma Perilaku Seksual Kaum Remaja: Sebuah Penelitian Terhadap Remaja Jakarta*. Jakarta: C. V. Rajawali.

Sheidlower, Jesse T. and Jonathan E. Lighter (1993). "A recent coinage (Not!)" *American Speech* 68: 213-218.

Simons, Gary F. (1982). "Word taboo and comparative Austronesian linguistics." In *Papers from the Third International Conference on Austronesian Linguistics*. Volume 3, edited by Amran Halim, Lois Carrington and Stephen A. Wurm. Canberra: Australian National University. Pacific Linguistics Series C-76, pp. 157-226.

Simonson, Douglas "Peppo" (1981). *Pidgin to da Max*. Honolulu: Bess Press.

St. John, Spencer (1863). *Life in the Forests of the Far East*. Volume 2. London: Smith, Elder, 2nd edition.

Suhadi, M. Agu (1989). *Humor itu Serius: Pengantar ke "Ilmu Humor."* Jakarta: Pustakakarya Grafikatama.

Suhardi (1977). "Permainan kata dalam Bahasa Jawa." *Bahasa dan Sastra* 6: 2-6.

Suharto (1983). "Bahasa walikan malang tidak lagi bersifat rahasia." *Sinar Harapan* (9 August).

Tannahill, Reay (1980). *Sex in History*. New York: Stein and Day.

Thompson, Stith (1993). *Motif-Index of Folk Literature: A Classification of Narrative Elements in Folk Tales, Ballads, Myths, Fables, Mediaeval Romances, Exempla, Fabliaux, Jest-Books, and Local Legends*. Bloomington: Indiana University Press, compact disk edition.

Thoolen, Hans, ed. (1987). *Indonesia and the Rule of Law: Twenty Years of "New Order" Government*. London: Frances Pinter.

Thorne, Tony (1990). *The Dictionary of Contemporary Slang: With More Than 5,000 Racy and Raffish Colloquial Expressions — from America, Great Britain, Australia, the Caribbean, and other English-speaking Places*. New York: Pantheon Books.

United States Department Of State (1993). *Country Reports on Human Rights Practices for 1992*. Washington, DC: U. S. Government Printing Office.

van der Meij, Th. C. (1983). *Enige aspecten van geheimtaal in Jakarta*. Bachelor's dissertation, University of Leiden, Netherlands. [cited in Rahardja and Chambert-Loir (1988) and in Chambert-Loir (1990)].

Wentworth, Harold and Stuart Berg Flexner (1975). *Dictionary of American Slang*. New York: Thomas Y. Crowell, 2nd edition.

Wilson, Edward O. (1975). *Sociobiology: The New Synthesis*. Cambridge, Massachusetts: Belknap Press of Harvard, .

Winstedt, Richard O. (1934). "A history of Negri Sembilan." *Journal of the Malayan Branch of the Royal Asiatic Society* 12, no. 3: 39-94.

Wolff, John U. and Soepomo Poedjosoedarmo (1982). *Communicative Codes in Central Java*. Linguistic Series VIII, Data Paper No.116, Ithaca, New York: Department of Asian Studies, Cornell University.

Tables

Table 1. Previously Unreported Prokem

Prokem	Indonesian Definition
cabarbut	cabut
culun	1. lucu (Rahardja & Chambert-Loir 1990: 53) 2. bodoh[b] 3. jelek
dokarku	1. mobil (Rahardja & Chambert-Loir 1990: 56) 2. dari[b] 3. darah[b]
monyarnyet	monyet
PPP	putera-puteri presiden[d]
pusarsing	pusing
RUSTAMAJI[c]	rusak tampang karena jigong
SUDARMAJI.	Sudah *dahar* , lima bayar *siji* [d]
SUDOMO.	Susu doi montok.
USDEK	1. "Udane soyo deres enake kelonan. (Hujan semakin lebat yang enak berdekapan.)" (Amien 1988: 58) 2. urusan dewek

[a]The definition following "**P=**" gives the meaning of the Prokem column. The meaning following "**I=**" gives the meaning of the Indonesian column.
[b]This is a previously unreported definition.
[d]*Dahar* is Javanese for "to eat." *Siji* is Javanese for "one."

Words and/or Definitions

English Definition[a]
to leave
1. funny 2. stupid 3. ugly
P=my horse cart, my dog cart; **I**=1. car 2. from 3. blood; descent
monkey, person (abusive)
P=*Partai Persatuan Pembangunan* (Islamic Political Party); **I**=president's sons and daughters (i.e. royal presidency)
dizzy
ugly face because of tartar
After eating, five [people] pay one.
[Her] breasts are plump.
P=*Undang-undang dasar 1945; Socialisme ala Indonesia; Demokrasi terpimpin; Ekonomi terpimpin; Kepribadian Indonesia* (the five principles of the late President Sukarno's government); **I**=1. The rain is heavier, it's nice to embrace. (now standard [Suhadi 1989: 55], unlikely to be true Prokem [Chambert-Loir, personal communication]) 2. one's own business

[c]Acronyms appear as all-capitals throughout the text. Acronym definitions are underlined to indicate derivation more so than usage, since some acronyms may be so commonly used that they are no longer considered as such, particularly those that have entered standard usage.

Table 2. Summary of Transformations

Name of Transformation[a]	Generative Grammar[b]
I. Ludlings	
A. Expansion	
1. Arbitrary	
a. Suffix to:	
i. Word	$W \rightarrow WX$
ii. Syllable	
(a) "ar" infix	$S_1 S_2 \ldots S_{n-1} L_{1,n} X \rightarrow$ $S_1 S_2 \ldots S_{n-1} L_{1,n} \underline{ar} L_{1,n} X$
(b) "in" infix	$S_1 S_2 \ldots S_{n-1} L_{1,n} X \rightarrow$ $S_1 S_2 \ldots S_{n-1} L_{1,n} \underline{in} X$
(c) "lah" infix	$S_1 S_2 \ldots S_n \rightarrow S_1 \underline{lah} S_2 \underline{lah} \ldots S_n \underline{lah}$
(d) "se" infix	$S_1 S_2 \ldots S_n \rightarrow$ $S_1 \underline{se} S_2 \underline{se} \ldots L_{n,m-1} \underline{se} L_{n,m}$
iii. Other	
(a) "arg" infix	$L_1 L_2 \ldots L_n \rightarrow L_1 \underline{arg} L_2 \ldots L_n$
(b) "ark" infix	$L_1 L_2 \ldots L_n \rightarrow L_1 \underline{ark} L_2 \ldots L_n$
(c) "ok" infix	$S_1 S_2 \ldots L_{1,m} X \rightarrow S_1 S_2 \ldots L_{1,m} \underline{ok} X$ $S_1 S_2 \ldots S_m X \rightarrow S_1 S_2 \ldots S_m \underline{ok} X$
b. Prefix to:	
i. Word	$W \rightarrow XW$
ii. Syllable	
iii. Final	
c. Prefix and suffix	
2. Conditioned	
a. Suffix to:	
i. Word	
ii. Syllable	$L_{1,1} V_{2,1} \ldots L_{n,1} L_{1,2} V_{2,2} \ldots L_{n,2} X \rightarrow$ $L_{1,1} V_{2,1} \ldots L_{n,1} L_x L_{1,2} V_{2,1} L_{2,2} \ldots$ $L_{n,2} L_x X$
iii. Nucleus/final	
b. Prefix to:	
i. Word	
ii. Syllable	

Code	Prokem Example
{SW}	not reported in Prokem [c]
{ar}	cabut → cabarbut
{in}	perek → pinerinek
{lah}	not recorded in Prokem
{se₁}	not recorded in Prokem
{arg}	not recorded in Prokem
{ark}	not recorded in Prokem
{ok₁}	berat → berokat
{ok₂}	diam → diokam [d]
{cong}	tipu → congtipu
{CSS}	not recorded in Prokem

65

Table 2. Summary of Transformations (continued)

Name of Transformation[a]	Generative Grammar[b]
iii. Final/nucleus	
B. Contraction	$S_1S_2\ldots S_n \to S_1S_2\ldots S_{n-1}$
C. Substitution	$S_1S_2\ldots S_n \to S_1S_2\ldots S_{n-1}\,X_n$
1. "ce" replacement	$S_1X \to S_1\underline{ce}$
2. "e" replacement	$XVY \to X\underline{e}Y$
3. "ong" replacement	$S_1S_2\ldots S_{n-1}L_{n,1}X \to$ $S_1S_2\ldots S_{n-1}L_{n,1}\underline{ong}$
4. "se" replacement	$S_1S_2\ldots S_{n-1}L_{n,1}X \to$ $S_1S_2\ldots S_{n-1}L_{n,1}\underline{se}$
D. Rearrangement	
1. Reversal	[indeterminate]
a. By phonemes/ graphemes	$XL_{1,m}L_{2,m}\ldots L_{n,m}Y \to$ $XL_{n,m}L_{n-1,m}\ldots L_{1,m}Y$
b. By syllables	$S_1S_2\ldots S_n \to S_nS_{n-1}\ldots S_1$
2. Transposition	[indeterminate]
a. Symmetric transposition	
i. Syllables	
ii. Initials	
(a)	$L_{1,1}L_{2,1}\ldots L_{n,1}L_{1,2}L_{2,2}\ldots L_{n,2} \to$ $L_{1,2}L_{2,1}\ldots L_{n,1}L_{1,1}L_{2,2}\ldots L_{n,2}$
(b)	$XS_1L_{1,2}Y \to XL_{1,2}S_1Y$
(c)	$L_{1,1}L_{2,1}L_{1,2}L_{2,2}X \to$ $L_{1,2}L_{2,2}L_{1,1}L_{2,1}X$
iii. Finals	
iv. Nuclei	$L_{1,1}L_{2,1}L_{1,2}L_{2,2}L_{2,3} \to$ $L_{1,1}L_{2,2}L_{1,2}L_{2,1}L_{2,3}$
b. Asymmetric transposition:	
i. Syllables	
ii. Initials and finals	
3. Shuffle	$L_1L_2\ldots L_n \to L_a\ldots L_yL_z$

Code	Prokem Example
{C}	amplop → amp
{S}	Astaga! → Astan!
{ce}	bule → bulce
{e}	majang → mejeng[e]
{ong}	lesbian → lesbong
{se$_2$}	murah → murse
{R}	biji → jibi
{Rp}	brengsek → brengkes
{Rs}	pergi → giper
{T}	satria → astria[d]
{Ti$_1$}	cabang → bacang
{Ti$_2$}	obat → bo'at
{Td}	kucing → cikung
{N}	cabut → cubat
{Sh}	mobil → bolim

Table 2. Summary of Transformations (continued)

Name of Transformation[a]	Generative Grammar[b]
E. Multiple transformations[f]	
1. Expansion + contraction	
(a) "ho" prefix + contraction	$S_1 S_2 \ldots S_n \, X \rightarrow \underline{ho}S_1 S_2 \ldots L_{n,1}$
(b) "ik" infix + contraction	$S_1 S_2 \ldots L_{1,m} XY \rightarrow S_1 S_2 \ldots L_{1,m} \underline{ik}X$
(c) "in" infix + contraction	$S_1 S_2 \ldots S_n \rightarrow S_1 \underline{in} S_2 \ldots S_{n-1}$
(d) "kos" prefix + contraction	$S_1 S_2 \ldots S_n \, X \rightarrow \underline{kos}S_1 S_2 \ldots L_{n,1}$
(e) "o" infix + contraction	$C_1 V_2 \ldots S_n \rightarrow C_1 \underline{o} V_2 \ldots S_{n-1}$
(f) "ok" infix + contraction	$S_1 S_2 \ldots L_{1,m} XY \rightarrow S_1 S_2 \ldots L_{1,m} \underline{ok}X$
(g) "se" infix + contraction	$S_1 S_2 \ldots S_n \rightarrow$ $S_1 \underline{se} S_2 \underline{se} \ldots L_{n,m-1} \underline{s}$
(h) "so" prefix + contraction	$S_1 S_2 \ldots S_n \rightarrow \underline{so}S_1 S_2 \ldots S_{n-1}$
2. Expansion + substitution	$S_1 S_2 \ldots S_n \rightarrow S_1 \underline{ok} S_2 \ldots S_{n-1} X$
3. Expansion + rearrangement	
(a) "ok" infix + transposition	$S_1 \ldots S_{m-1} L_{1,m} L_{2,m} \ldots L_{n,m} X \rightarrow$ $S_1 \ldots S_{m-1} \underline{ok} L_{n,m} L_{n-1,m} \ldots L_{1,m} X$
(b) Syllabic reversal + "si" infix	$S_1 S_2 \rightarrow S_2 \underline{si} S_1$
4. Expansion + rearrangement + substitution	
5. Expansion + rearrangement + contracting	$S_1 \ldots S_{m-1} L_{1,m} L_{2,m} \ldots L_{n,m} S_{m+1} \ldots S_q \rightarrow$ $S_1 \ldots S_{m-1} L_{n,m} \underline{ok} L_{n-1,m} \ldots L_{1,m} S_{m+1} \ldots S_{q-1}$

68

Code	Prokem Example
{ho}	kemeja → hokem[d]
{ik+C}	pemancar → pemikancar → pemikan[d]
{in+C}	banci → binanci → binan
{kos}	mobil → kosmob
{o+C}	dia → d'oia → d'oi
{ok$_2$+C}	durian → dokurian → dokur
{se$_1$+C}	not recorded in Prokem
{so+C}	not recorded in Prokem
{ok$_1$+S}	beli → bokeli → bokal
{ok$_1$+Ts$_1$}	akta → akokta → akokat[d]
{Rs+si}	cabut → butsica
{ok$_2$+Ts$_1$+C}	leher → lekoher → lekor

Table 2. Summary of Transformations (continued)

Name of Transformation[a]	Generative Grammar[b]
6. Rearrangement + contraction[g]	[indeterminate]
II. Old word given new meaning (e.g. euphemism or pun)[h]	(not applicable)
III. Acronyms[h]	(not applicable)
IV. Acronym + new meaning[h]	(not applicable)
V. Unknown transformation	(not applicable)

[a]Transformation categories are after Laycock (1972).

[b]Symbols in the generative grammar are as follows: C_n = nth consonant cluster of word; L_n = nth letter or consonant cluster of word; $L_{n,m}$ = nth letter or consonant cluster of mth syllable in word, V_n = nth vowel of word; $V_{n,m}$ = nth vowel of mth syllable in word; S_n = nth syllable of word; W = word; X, Y = any word part. Finals (i.e., the actual letters of a word) in the generative grammars are lower-case and underlined. Non-finals (i.e., symbols) are upper case. When no generative grammar is given, then the transformation is apparently not used in Prokem.

[c]Non-Prokem generative grammars are given for Indonesian and Malaysian ludlings described in Table 2.

[d]This transformation has only been reported by Amien (1988) or Pur (1989), and has not been recorded by Rahardja and Chambert-Loir (1988; 1990).

Code	Prokem Example
{T+C}	jahit → ja'it → ajit[d]
{O}	abang
{_}	ABG → anak baru gede
{_+O}	ABIDIN → atas biaya dinas
{?}	selon ⇒ jagoan

[e]This transformation occurs also in Javanese in which the letter "a" is changed to "e" for many words, and is indicative informal speech (Horne 1974: xvi). Such a transformation may also exist for other languages, such as Balinese, that form the substrate for the Jakartan dialect. A subset of this transformation also occurs in a sub-dialect of Jakartanese where a final /a/ sound is changed to an /e/ sound (Lumintaintang 1981: 6). The {e} transformation is only noted in this dictionary when the {e}-transformed word does not exist as a formal word in Indonesian, Javanese, Sundanese, or Balinese dictionaries, and when it is not a transformation from a final /a/ sound.

[f]The codes given in this table for multiple transformations are not exhaustive for those that occur in the dictionaries, but are merely representative.

[g]This kind of transformation is not listed in Laycock (1972).

[h]This is not a ludic transformation, and hence is not in Laycock (1972).

Table 3. Some Prokem Words of English

Prokem	Indonesian Definition[a]
beriwait	berak (Rahardja & Chambert-Loir 1990: 44) {O}
caplin	bego (Rahardja & Chambert-Loir 1990: 50) {O}
CHICAGO	Cikini, Kali Pasir, Gondangdia Lama (Rahardja & Chambert-Loir 1990: 161) {_+O}
hombre	homo (Rahardja & Chambert-Loir 1990: 64) {S/O}
OPEC	"Organisasi Pedagang Ekonomi Cukupan" (Rahardja & Chambert-Loir 1990: 166) {_+O}
pakalolo	ganja (Rahardja & Chambert-Loir 1990: 92) {O}
ponsterling	bapak yang galak (Rahardja & Chambert-Loir 1988: 50) {O}
Swiss	Minang[c] {O}

[a]Codes enclosed by braces {} refer to transformations defined in Table 2.
[b]The definition following "**P=**" gives the meaning of the Prokem column. The definition following "**I=**" gives the meaning of the Indonesian column.

English Definition[b]

P=U.S. singer, Barry White; I=to shit (compare to the English rhyming slang, "Richard the Third", meaning turd [Thorne 1990: 425])

P=Charlie Chaplin?; I=stupid

P=Chicago, Illinois; I=three street names in Jakarta that form a triangular area and may have been a gang territory (Chambert-Loir, personal communication)

P=hombre (probably reinforced from imported U.S. Western films and/or a brand of jeans [Chambert-Loir, personal communication); I=homo [from the Prokem *hombreng* derived from *homo brengsek* "useless homo", probably reinforced from the English/Spanish

P=Organization of Petroleum Exporting Countries; I=Organization of Economic Traders [providing] Just Enough

P=*Pakalolo* is Hawaiian Pidgin English for ganja (Simonson 1981; Nash 1992: 266), probably from Hawaiian: *paka*, "park" + *lolo*, "brain" (Pukui, Elber, & Mookini 1975: 91,130). It was likely introduced to Indonesia by surfers (e.g. see Cralle 1991: 28,58, 181-182).]; I=ganja (*Cannabis* spp.)

P=Pound Sterling; I=father who is mean/fierce

P=Swiss; I=Minangkabau (a region of Sumatra), Minangkabauese

[c]Definitions without references were reported in more than one published source.

Table 4. Prokem Words Indicating a North

Prokem	Source Language	Indonesian Definition[a]
JADEL	—	Jawa Deli[c] {_}
JAKON	—	Jawa Kontrak[c] {_}
da'e	adek (Medan/Deli dialect of Indonesian)	adik (Pur 1989: 24) {Ti$_2$+C}
CABO	cabe mudo (Minang-kabauese)	cabe muda (Rahardja & Chambert-Loir 1988: 86) {_}

[a]Codes enclosed by braces {} refer to transformations defined in Table 2.

[b]The definition following "**P=**" gives the meaning of the Prokem column. The definition following "**I=**" gives the meaning of the Indonesian column.

[c]Definitions without references were reported in more than one published source.

Sumatran Origin or Influence

English Definition[b]

I=person from a Javanese resettlement area in Deli

I=Javanese Contract (referring to the Javanese resettlement scheme in Deli)

I=younger sibling

P=whore; **I**="young hot pepper" (implying someone from Minangkabau)

Table 5. Summary of Ludlings from Indonesia,

Base Language(s)	Ludling Name[a]	Location[b]	Speech Group
Jakartan	Prokem	Jakarta	students, criminals
Jakartan		Jakarta	homosexuals
Jakartan	Bencong	Jakarta	transvestites, transsexuals
Indonesian		Indonesia	
Indonesian		Indonesia	
Indonesian	Balik?	Indonesia	
Indonesian	Balik	Indonesia	
Indonesian, Javanese	Walikan	Malang (East Java Province)	literates
Javanese	Walikan [2 kinds]	eastern Java	children
Javanese		Solo (Central Java Province)	ages 10-15
Javanese		Solo (Central Java Province)	ages 10-15
Javanese	Walikan Aksara	eastern Java	children
Javanese		Surakarta (East Java Province)	female court servants
Javanese		Kebumen (Central Java)	
Javanese		eastern Java	children

Malaysia and Brunei

Dates[c]	Transformation Method[d]	Citations
1960s?-1950s?-?	{P}	Oemarjati (1980)[4], Dreyfuss (1983); Amien (1988); Rahardja and Chambert-Loir (1988; 1990); Pur (1989)
<1983-?	{CSS}	van der Meij (1983); Rahardja and Chambert-Loir (1988: 8); Chambert-Loir (1990: 82)
<1986-	{ong}	Atmojo (1986: 10-11); Chambert-Loir (1990: 83)
<1983-?	{CSS}	Chambert-Loir (1984: 109)
<1983-?	{arg/ark}	Chambert-Loir (1984: 109)
<1983-?	{Ts}	Chambert-Loir (1984: 109)
<1939-?	{Ts}	Chambert-Loir (1990: 83)
1930s?-[e]	{Rp}[f]	Suharto (1983)
<1971-?	{Rp}	Sadtono (1971: 32,35,38); Chambert-Loir (1984: 109)
<1921-?	{Rs}	Jasawijata and Kartadarmadja (1921); Suhardi (1977: 3)
<1921-?	{Ti₁}	Jasawijata and Kartadarmadja (1921); Suhardi (1977: 3)
<1971-?	{S}	Sadtono (1971: 32,36-38); Chambert-Loir (1984: 109)
<1921-?	{CSS}	Jasawijata and Kartadarmadja (1921); Suhardi (1977: 3)
<1921-?	{in+C}[g]	Jasawijata and Kartadarmadja (1921); Suhardi (1977: 3)
c. 1958	{so+C}	Chambert-Loir (1990: 82)

---

[4] Oemarjati (1980) analyzed graffiti in Jakarta, which mainly included acronyms but also included some Prokem words, e.g., "jabu" = Indonesian "baju" = English "shirt", "laming" = Indonesian "maling" = English "thief".

77

Table 5. Summary of Ludlings from Indonesia,

Base Language(s)	Ludling Name[a]	Location[b]	Speech Group
Javanese	Tjekakan	eastern Java	children
Javanese		Tegal (Central Java Province)	students
Javanese	Seselan	Kediri (East Java Province)	students
Sundanese		West Java Province	
Minang-kabauese	[2 kinds]	West Sumatra Province	
Bengkuluese		South Sumatra Province	
Makassarese		South Sulawesi Province	
Malay	Cakap Balik	Linggi (Negri Sembilan State)	children
Malay		Negri Sembilan State	Children
Malay		Kedah (Wellesley State)	children
Malay	Bahasa Rahsia	Johor State	children
Malay	Balik	Brunei	royal court women
Timugon Murut		Sabah	
Timugon Murut		Sabah	
Timugon Murut	[2 kinds]	Sabah	

78

Malaysia and Brunei (continued)

Dates[c]	Transformation Method[d]	Citations
<1971-?	{C}[h]	Sadtono (1971: 32,34-35,38); Laycock (1972: 77-78)
<1977-?	{arg/ark}	Suhardi (1977: 4-5); Chambert-Loir (1984: 109)
c. 1958-?	{CSS}	Sadtono (1971: 32-34,38); Suhardi (1977: 4-5); Chambert-Loir (1984: 109); Chambert-Loir (1990: 82)
	{CSS}	Chambert-Loir (1984: 109)
	{CSS}	Chambert-Loir (1984: 109)
	{CSS}	Suhardi (1977: 5)
<1988-?	?	Chambert-Loir (1990: 82)
<1917-?	{P}	Evans (1917: 115); Evans (1923: 276-277); Laycock (1972: 81)
<1917-?	{Ts}[i]	Evans (1917: 116); Laycock (1972: 84)
<1917-?	?	Evans (1917: 115); Evans (1923: 277)
c. 1995	{Ti}	Rahman (1995)
<1862-?	{lah}[j]	St. John (1863: 289); Laycock (1972: 70)
<1972-	{C}	Laycock (1972: 78,94), Prentice (1982)
<1982-	{Ts}	Prentice (1982)
<1982-	{SW}	Prentice (1982)

[a]*Balik*, *Balikan*, and *Walikan* all mean "reverse", e.g. more properly *Bahasa Balikan* means "reverse language."

[b]Specific locations are given when known, but do not preclude the possibility of wider use.

[c]Most papers give little data, particularly about the dates of existence of the ludling. Consequently, the date of publication is often used here as a point of reference.

[d]Transformation methods that occur in Prokem are given in **bold**, but may not match Prokem exactly in implementation. {P} indicates polysystemic transformations.

[e]Suharto (1983) estimated that Walikan originated 50 years prior to publication (1930s), a more definitive date that he gave was 15 years before publication (i.e., 1968).

[f]The predominant Walikan transformation is reversal by letters {Rp}, but there are many exceptions and hence the language is actually polysystemic {P}.

[g]This transformation in Javanese is different than as it occurs in Prokem. The Javanese transformation truncates the first syllable, whereas the Prokem transformation truncates the last syllable.

[h]This is a different form of contraction than reported by Jasawijata and Kartadarmadja (1921).

[i]This may be asymmetric.

[j]The description of this ludling is based on a single example given by St. John (mari→malahrilah), but he notes that there were actually several dynamic systems (1863: 289).

***Table 6. Cakap Balik: Peninsular Malaysian
Negri Sembilan State)[a]***

Indonesian/ Malaysian	Prokem	Cakap Balik
anak	naak[c]	nahak
banyak	nyabak[c]	nyabak
besok	sebok[c]	sebok
lebih/lebeh	belih (Pur 1989: 13)	beleh
makan	kaman[c]	kaman
minggu	guming (Amien 1988:17)	guming
pergi	giper[c]	giper
tinggi	giting[c]	giting

[a]Cakap Balik data is from Evans (1917: 115; 1923: 276-277).
[b]Codes enclosed by braces { } refer to transformations defined in Table 2.
[c]Prokem words without references were reported in more than one published source.

Ludling Words that Appear in Prokem (from

Transformation[b]	Other Prokem transformations for this word?	English
$\{Ti_1\}$	no	child
$\{Ti_1+C\}$	no	much, a lot
$\{Ti_1\}$	no	tomorrow
$\{Ti_1\}$	no	more
$\{Ti_1\}$	yes	to eat
$\{Rs\}$	no	week, Sunday
$\{Rs\}$	yes	to go
$\{RS\}$	no	high (meaning "intoxicated" in Prokem)

Table 7. Prokem Words that Are Both Puns and

Prokem	Indonesian Definition[a]
cungki	kunci (Amien 1988: 10) {Ti$_1$+S/O}
genggong	ganggu (Pur 1989: 36) {e+ong/O}
hombre	[see Table 3]
kencana	kencing (Pur 1989: 55) {S/O}
keong	kaya (Pur 1989: 56) {e+ong/O}
kelapa	kepala {Ti$_1$/O}[c]
lepokit	lepit [lipat] (Pur 1989: 69) {ok$_1$/O}
lingsang	langsing (Amien 1988: 28) {N/O}
maharani	marah (Pur 1989: 74) {S/O}
mode	dame [damai] (Pur 1989: 74) {Ti$_1$+S/O}
ramah	1. marah (Pur 1989: 98) {Ti$_1$/O} 2. "rajin menjamah" (Amien 1988: 44) {O}
rebak	berak[c] {Ti$_1$/O}
sipil	sepele[c] {S/O}
tanggung	gantung (Pur 1989: 115) {Ti$_1$+S/O}

English Definition[b]
P=[*cungkil* is crowbar (which could be used as a "key" by burglars)]; **I**=key
P=Jew's harp, harmonica; **I**=to annoy, to trouble [see Table 3]
P=gold; **I**=urine [In English slang, to give someone a "golden shower" is to urinate upon them for sexual gratification (Chapman 1986: 172). In English folklore, an analogy between shit and gold is more common (Legman 1975: 917-920).]
P=snail; spiral; **I**=rich
P=coconut; **I**=head[d,e]
P=*lepok* is misfold; **I**=fold
P=linsang (*Prionodon linsang*) [k.o. civet] (the linsang is slender and is probably seen pacing in the zoo by Jakartans); **I**=1. slender 2. shrill 3. to go back and forth[d]
P=maharani; **I**=anger, angry
P=mode, fashion; **I**=peace
P=friendly; **I**=1. anger, angry 2. to fondle (literally, "to touch diligently")
P=deep wound; **I**=shit, to shit
P=civil, civilian; **I**=trivial, worthless (This may refer to the dominance of the military in Indonesian society [e.g. see Dalton 1991: 17-18].)
P=1. guaranteed 2. insufficient 3. ill-timed; **I**=1. to hang 2. to depend on

[a]Codes enclosed by braces { } refer to transformations defined in Table 2.

[b]The definition following "**P**=" gives the meaning of the Prokem column. The definition following "**I**=" gives the meaning of the Indonesian column.

[c]Definitions without references were reported in more than one published source.

[d]These words are possibly linguistic transformations within Indonesian, i.e. transformations pre-dating Prokem.

[e]"Coconut" and "head" are linked in myth over a wide geographic area (motif A2611.3 in Thompson 1993; see also Wentworth and Flexner 1975: 113).

Table 8. Words Used in the Underworld of

Prokem	Indonesian[a,b]
gajo	**jago** (Pur 1989: 33) {Ti$_1$}
gorang	**garong** (Amien 1988: 16) {N}
jeger	1. bandit; preman[c]
	2. **jago**[c]
	3. tukang pukul[c] {O}
jokag	**jago** (Pur 1989: 49) {ok$_1$+C}
selon	"1. **jago**an
	2. mengajak berantem
	3. goyang-goyang" (Rahardja &
	Chambert-Loir 1990: 100) {?}

[a]The words in **boldface** were used in the underworld. The Prokem words were not known to have been used; these words are from Cribb (1991: 18).

[b]Codes enclosed by braces { } refer to transformations defined in Table 2.

[c]Definitions without references were reported in more than one published source.

Colonial Batavia

Archaic Meaning	Current Meaning
labor boss	gamecock; leader
brigand	thief
labor boss	1. bandit; street kid
	2. gamecock; leader
	3. hourly worker
labor boss	gamecock; leader
labor boss	1. gamecock; leader
	2. to ask for a fight
	3. shakiness

Table 9. Prokem Words that Indicate an

Prokem	Indonesian[a]
cangkul	1. masuk sekolah 2. bekerja (Rahardja & Chambert-Loir 1990: 161) {O}
gaji	bandit (Amien 1989: 14) {O/S+O}
ladang	kawasan gang[b] {O}
mbah	dukun klenik[b] {O}
pacul	bekerja (Rahardja & Chambert-Loir 1990: 91) {O}
sawah	bekerja (Rahardja & Chambert-Loir 1990: 100) {O}

[a]Codes enclosed by braces { } refer to transformations defined in Table 2.

[b]Definitions without references were reported in more than one published source.

Origin in Rural Banditry

Literal Meaning of Prokem	Literal Meaning of Indonesian
mattock (kind of farm tool)	1. to enter school 2. to work
salary	bandit
a gang's territory	unirrigated farmland
1. leader, champion 2. stronghold 3. form of address	entranced shaman (many criminals in the outskirts of colonial Batavia had shamanic knowledge [Cribb 1991: 19-20])
hoe	to work
k.o. rice field	to work

Table 10. Words in Prokem that Refer to

Prokem	Indonesian Definition[a]
askis	siksa (Amien 1988: 2) {Rp}
bantai	siksa[c] {O}
dibon	dipukul, disiksa dalam penjara[c] {O}
lasah	salah[c] {Ti$_1$}

[a]Codes enclosed by braces { } refer to transformations defined in Table 2.

[b]The definition following "**P=**" gives the meaning of the Prokem column. The definition following "**I=**" gives the meaning of the Indonesian column.

[c]Definitions without references were reported in more than one published source.

Torture

English Definition[b]
torture
P=to butcher meat; **I**=torture
P=endebted; **I**=tortured in jail/prison. This probably refers to the widespread torture and corruption in jails; it is not unheard of to be able to bribe one's way out of a jail (Thoolen 1987: 197).
P=1. to torture 2. to strike 3. to exhaust oneself 4. to spread flat 5. work clothes; **I**=error; guilty

Table 11. Words in Prokem for Film

Prokem	Indonesian Definition[a]
2-6	blue film (B=2, F=6), BF[c] {O}
Bentoel Filter	blue film, BF, film porno[c] {_}
bokep	1. pilem biru (blue film) [Rahardja and Chambert-Loir 1990: 46] {ok$_1$+S} 2. bopeng[c] {ok$_1$+R+C}
Botol Fanta	BF, blue film, film porno[c] {_}
Jakarta-Bogor	blue film (nomor polisi kendaraan: Jakarta = B, Bogor = F)[c] {O}
lepem	pilem [film] (Rahardja & Chambert-Loir 1990: 78) {e+Ti$_1$}
lipem	pilem [film][c] {Ti$_1$}
sorot	film (Amien 1988: 52) {O}
unyil	blue film (BF) [Rahardja and Chambert-Loir 1990: 111] {O}

[a]Codes enclosed by braces { } refer to transformations defined in Table 2.

[b]The definition following "**P=**" gives the meaning of the Prokem column. The definition following "**I=**" gives the meaning of the Indonesian column.

[c]Definitions without references were reported in more than one source.

English Definition[b]
blue movie, pornographic film
P=k.o. cigarette; **I**=blue movie (pornographic film). This is a possible reference to fellatio. [Compare to the English slang, "smoker" for stag film (Di Lauro & Rabkin (1976: 25)]
1. pornographic film 2. pock-marked
P=k.o. soft drink; **I**=blue movie; pornographic film
P=names of two cities on Java; **I**=blue movie (pornographic film) [derived from the license plates on police vehicles in those cities]
film
film
P=light ray; **I**=film
P="Si Unyil" was the name of a popular character in a 1980s children's television show (Chambert-Loir, personal communiciation); **I**=pornographic film

About the Author

Thomas H. Slone is a staff scientist at the University of California at Berkeley, where he has published more than 30 papers in the field of cancer research over the past 17 years. He has traveled extensively, and has visited Iindonesia five times.

He has translated and edited a monumental two-volume collection of Papua New Guinean folktales, *One Thousand One Papua New Guinean Nights*. He has written the article, "Tok nogut: An introduction to malediction in Papua New Guinea" (*Maledicta: The International Journal of Verbal Aggression* 11: 75-104, 1996), and he is a major contributor to a revision of a Tok Pisin-English dictionary.

Masalai Press

Masalai Press is a publisher specializing in Pacific Island and Asian folklore. Other titles published by Masalai Press are:

- *One Thousand One Papua New Guinean Nights: Folktales from Wantok Newspaper. Volume 1: Tales from 1972-1985.* Edited and translated by Thomas H. Slone. 528 pages, 8-1/4 by 11 inches. ISBN 0-9714127-0-7.

- *One Thousand One Papua New Guinean Nights: Folktales Stories from Wantok Newspaper. Volume 2: Tales from 1986-1997, Indices, Glossary, References, and Maps.* Edited and translated by Thomas H. Slone. 613 pages, 8-1/4 by 11 inches. ISBN 0-9714127-1-5.

- *Rasta Is Cuss: A Dictionary of Rastafarian Cursing* by Thomas H. Slone. 108 pages, 5 by 8 inches. ISBN 0-9714127-4-X.

Masalai Press takes its name from the malevolent spirits of Papua New Guinea. These spirits can be associated with a specific location (such as a mountain) or specific natural feature (such as a whirlpool). In a human-like (anthropomorphic) form, a *masalai* is often a large and/or ugly cannibal, similar to an ogre.

www.ingramcontent.com/pod-product-compliance
Lightning Source LLC
Chambersburg PA
CBHW021343090426
42742CB00008B/727